Name _____

My Cat

My cat is black.

She likes to play.

1. ___ — — — cat is black.

2. My ___ — — — — is black.

3. My cat is — — — — — — ___.

4. ___ — — — — likes to play.

5. She likes to — — — — — ___.

6. My ___ — — — — is ___ — — — — .

   She ___ — — — — — to ___ — — — — — .

1

FS-32043 Reading

School

I go to school.

School is fun.

Good morning.

1. __ go to school.

2. I ___ to school.

3. I go to _____.

4. _____ is fun.

5. School is ____.

6. I ___ to _____.

School ___ fun.

Name _____

Jane Jumps

Jane can jump.

She can jump ten times.

1. _____ can jump.

2. Jane can _____.

3. She _____ jump ten times.

4. She can jump _____ times.

5. She can jump ten _____.

6. _____ can _____.

She _____ jump _____ times.

FS-32043 Reading

Name _____

Bugs

For lunch!

Pam likes bugs.

She likes red bugs.

1. _____ likes bugs.

2. Pam _____ bugs.

3. Pam likes _____.

4. _____ likes red bugs.

5. She likes _____ bugs.

6. _____ likes _____.

She _____ red _____.

4

Name _____

Tom's Dog

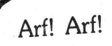

Tom has a big dog.
The dog sleeps with Tom.

1. _____ has a big dog.

2. Tom has a ____ dog.

3. Tom has a big ____ .

4. The dog _____ with Tom.

5. The dog sleeps ____ Tom.

6. _____ has _ big ____ .

The ____ sleeps _____ Tom.

FS-32043 Reading

Name _____

Jets

Jets are planes.

They go very fast.

Look!

1. _____ are planes.

2. Jets _ _ _ _ _ planes.

3. Jets are _ _ _ _ _ _ _ _ _ .

4. They _ _ _ _ very fast.

5. They go very _ _ _ _ _ _ .

6. _ _ _ _ _ _ are _ _ _ _ _ _ _ .

They _ _ _ _ very _ _ _ _ _ _ .

FS-32043 Reading

Name _____

The Ball

Jim has a ball.

It is yellow and red.

1. _____ has a ball.

2. Jim _____ a ball.

3. Jim has a _____.

4. It _____ yellow and red.

5. It is _____ and red.

6. _____ has _____ ball.

It _____ yellow _____ red.

FS-32043 Reading

Balloons

Ted has three balloons.

The balloons are red.

1. _____ has three balloons.

2. Ted _____ three balloons.

3. Ted has _____ balloons.

4. The _____ are red.

5. The balloons are _____ .

6. _____ has _____ balloons.

The _____ are _____ .

Name _____

Ice Cream

Ice cream is good.

It is very cold.

1. _____ _____ is good.

2. Ice cream ____ good.

Oh, this is good!

3. Ice cream is _____ .

4. ____ is very cold.

5. It is very _____ .

6. _____ cream ____ good.

It ____ very _____ .

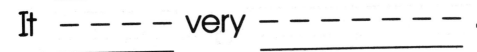

FS-32043 Reading

The Train

Nan has a toy train.

She plays with it every day.

I like my doll too!

1. ____has a toy train.

2. Nan has a ____train.

3. Nan has a toy ____.

4. She ____with it every day.

5. She plays with it ____day.

6. ____ has ___ toy ____.

She ____ with ___ every ____.

FS-32043 Reading

Name _____

A Pet

Jill has a pet duck.

The duck is white and yellow.

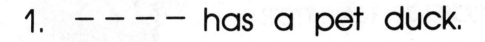

1. _ _ _ _ has a pet duck.

2. Jill has a _ _ _ _ duck.

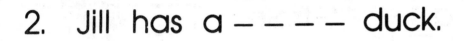

3. Jill has a pet _ _ _ _ _ _ _ .

4. The duck is _ _ _ _ _ _ _ _ and yellow.

5. The duck is white and _ _ _ _ _ _ _ .

6. _ _ _ _ _ _ has _ _ _ pet _ _ _ _ _ _ _ .

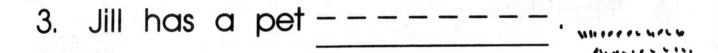

The duck is _ _ _ _ _ _ and _ _ _ _ _ _ .

FS-32043 Reading

Cookies

Bill made cookies.

The cookies were very good.

1. _____ made cookies.

2. Bill _____ cookies.

3. Bill made _____ .

4. The cookies were _____ good.

5. The cookies were very _____ .

6. _____ made _____ .

The _____ were _____ good.

FS-32043 Reading

Name _____

Books

I love to read!

I like books.
Books are fun for me.

1. _ _ like books.

2. I _ _ _ _ books.

3. I like _ _ _ _ _ .

4. _ _ _ _ _ _ _ _ are fun for _ _ _ .

5. Books _ _ _ _ fun _ _ _ _ me.

6. I _ _ _ _ _ books.

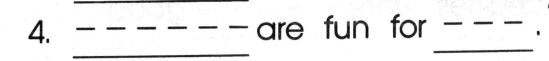

_ _ _ _ _ _ are _ _ _ _ for _ _ _ .

FS-32043 Reading

Name _____

A Plant

Jane has a plant.

It is green.

I like my plant.

1. _____ has a plant.

2. Jane _____ a plant.

3. Jane has a _____.

4. _____ is green.

5. It is _____.

6. _____ has __ plant.

_____ is _____.

Name _____

Hide and Seek

Dan and Mary play hide and seek.
They hide in the room.

1. Dan and _____ play hide and seek.

2. Dan and Mary _____ hide and seek.

3. Dan and Mary play _____ and seek.

4. They hide _____ the room.

5. They hide in the _____ .

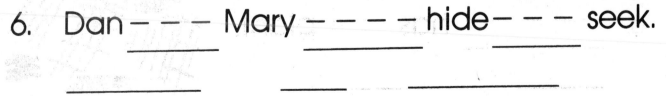

6. Dan _____ Mary _____ hide _____ seek.

_____ hide _____ the _____ .

FS-32043 Reading

Name _____

My Boat

I have a little boat.

I float it in the water.

1. I _ _ _ _ _ _ a little boat.

2. I have a _ _ _ _ _ _ boat.

3. I have a _ _ _ _ _ _ _ _ _ _ _ _.

4. I _ _ _ _ _ _ _ _ it in the water.

5. I float it in the _ _ _ _ _ _ _.

6. I _ _ _ _ _ _ a _ _ _ _ _ _ boat.

_ _ float _ _ in _ _ _ _ water.

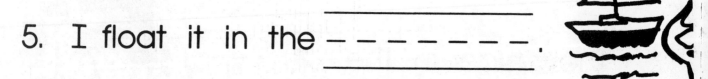

FS-32043 Reading

Name _____

The Green Car

Look!

I saw a little green car.
It went up the street.

1. I _____ a little green car.

2. I saw a _____ green _____.

3. It _____ up the _____.

4. It went __ the street.

5. It went up ___ street.

6. I __ a _____ green ___.

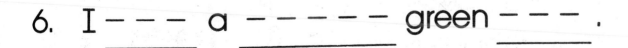

It _____ up ___ street.

17

FS-32043 Reading

The Doll

Tim has a doll.

It is his very best friend.

1. _____ has a doll.

2. Tim _____ a doll.

3. Tim has a _____.

4. It is _____ very best friend.

5. It is his _____ best _____.

6. _____ has _____ doll.

   _____ is _____ very _____ friend.

Name _____

Colors

Colors make things pretty.

I like blue and red best.

1. _____ – – – – – – make things pretty.

2. Colors – – – – – things pretty.

3. Colors make – – – – – – pretty.

4. I – – – – blue and red best.

5. I like – – – – and red best.

6. – – – – – – make – – – – – – pretty.

___ like – – – – and – – – best.

FS-32043 Reading

Name _____

My Monster

My monster has a big blue hat.
The hat has a rose on it.

Hi there!

1. What does my monster have?
_____
_____

2. Is it big or little?
_____
_____

3. What color is the hat?
_____
_____

4. Does the hat have a cat on it?
_____
_____

5. What does the hat have on it?
_____
_____

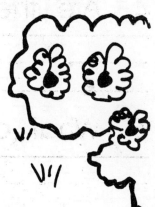

20

Name _____

Seeds

I planted four seeds.
Now they are big green plants.

1. What did I plant?

_____
_ _ _ _ _ _ _ _ _ _
_____

2. How many did I plant?

_____
_ _ _ _ _ _ _ _ _ _

3. Are the plants big?

_____
_ _ _ _ _ _ _ _ _ _

4. Are the plants red?

_____
_ _ _ _ _ _ _ _ _ _
_____

5. What color are the plants?

_____
_ _ _ _ _ _ _ _ _ _
_____

FS-32043 Reading

Name _____

Blocks

Jim plays with big blocks.
He does not make boats.
He just makes trains and trucks.

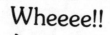
Wheeee!!

1. Who plays with blocks?

_____

_____

2. Are the blocks big or little?

_____

_____

3. Does Jim make boats?

_____

_____

4. Does Jim make houses?

_____

_____

5. What does Jim make?

_____

_____

Name _____

Mice

Jane saw some mice.

They were gray.

They were so cute!

They ate cheese and cookies.

1. What did Jane see?

   _____
   _____

2. Were the mice white?

   _____
   _____

3. Were the mice gray?

   _____
   _____

4. Did the mice eat cheese?

   _____
   _____

5. Did the mice eat cookies?

   _____

FS-32043 Reading

The Monkey

The monkey has fun.
He plays all day.
He is in the zoo.

1. Who is the story about?

_____

_____

2. Does the monkey have fun?

_____

_____

3. Does the monkey play?

_____

_____

4. When does the monkey play?

_____

_____

5. Where is the monkey?

_____

_____

munch
munch

How cute!

Name _____

The Elephant

The elephant is big and gray.

His trunk is long.

His ears are wide.

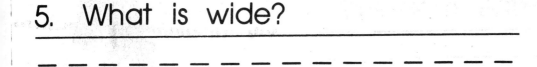

1. Who is the story about?

_____

_____

2. Is the elephant big or little?

_____

_____

3. What color is the elephant?

_____

_____

4. What is long?

_____

_____

5. What is wide?

_____

_____

FS-32043 Reading

Name _____

Bill's Bike

Bill has a new bike.
It has two wheels.
It is blue.

1. Who has a bike?

    _____

    _____

2. Is the bike old or new?

    _____

    _____

3. Does the bike have three wheels?

    _____

    _____

4. How many wheels does the bike have?

    _____

    _____

5. What color is the bike?

    _____

    _____

FS-32043 Reading

The Clown

A clown came to school.

She came on Monday.

She had six balloons.

1. Who came to school?

   _____

   _____

2. What day did she come?

   _____

   _____

3. Was the clown a boy?

   _____

   _____

4. How many balloons are there?

   _____

   _____

5. What did the clown have?

   _____

   _____

Name _____

Nan's Hamster

Nan has a brown hamster.

The hamster has a little wheel.

Nan loves her hamster.

1. Who has a hamster?

_____

_____

2. What color is the hamster?

_____

_____

3. Who has a wheel?

_____

_____

4. Is the wheel big or little?

_____

_____

5. Who loves the hamster?

_____

_____

FS-32043 Reading

Name _____

Our Cat

Our brown cat ran away.
She came back after five days.
I was so glad!

1. What color is our cat?
_____
_____

2. What did our cat do?
_____
_____

3. Did she come back after ten days?
_____
_____

4. Did she come back after four days?
_____
_____

5. After how many days did she come back?
_____
_____

Name _____

Sue's Snake

Sue has a pet snake.
It is in a green box.
The box has a top.

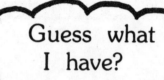

1. Who has a pet?

_____

_____

2. What is the pet?

_____

_____

3. Is the pet in a tree?

_____

_____

4. What color is the box?

_____

_____

5. Does the box have a top?

_____

_____

FS-32043 Reading

Name _____

A Game

Bob and Bill played a ball game.

They played at the park.

They played on Saturday.

1. Who played with Bob?

2. What did they play?

_____

3. Where did they play?

_____

4. Did they play on Monday?

_____

5. When did they play?

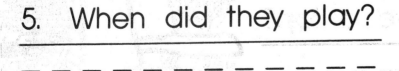

FS-32043 Reading

Joe's Lunch

Joe ate a red apple.

It was in his big lunch box.

Yum, yum!

I like apples!

1. Who ate something?

_____

_____

2. What color was it?

_____

_____

3. What did Joe eat?

_____

_____

4. Was Joe's lunch box little?

_____

_____

5. Was Joe's lunch box big?

_____

FS-32043 Reading

Name _____

The Park

John went to a park.

He played on the swings.

He jumped in the pool.

He did not go on the slide.

1. Is John a boy or a girl?

_____

_____

2. Where did John go?

_____

_____

3. Did he play on the slide?

_____

_____

4. What did he play on?

_____

_____

5. Where did he jump?

_____

_____

Skates

I have skates.
I skate every day.
I skate at school.
I skate at home.
I do not skate in the park.

whoopeeeeee!

1. What do I have?
_____
_____

2. When do I skate?
_____
_____

3. Do I skate at school?
_____
_____

4. Do I skate in the park?
_____
_____

5. Do I skate at home?
_____
_____

Name _____

Peter Pig

Peter Pig lives on a farm.

He is pink.

He is fat.

He eats apples.

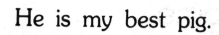
He is my best pig.

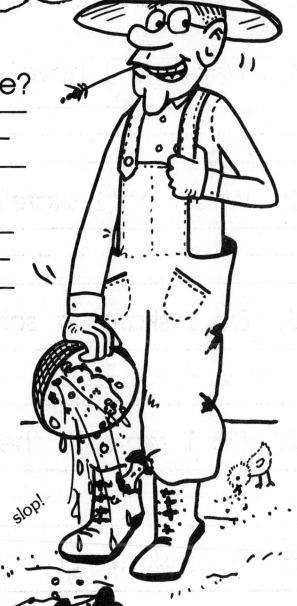
slop!

1. What is the pig's name?
_____
_____

2. Where does he live?
_____
_____

3. What color is he?
_____
_____

4. Is he fat or thin?
_____
_____

5. What does he eat?
_____
_____

35

FS-32043 Reading

Name _____

Jack's Bug

Jack ran in the park.

He ran after a lightning bug.

The little bug hid in the grass.

Jack looked and looked.

But he did not find it.

1. Where did Jack run?

   _____

   -

   _____

2. What did Jack do?

   _____

   -

   _____

3. Was the bug big or little?

   _____

   -

   _____

4. Where did the bug hide?

   _____

   -

   _____

5. Who looked and looked?

   _____

   -

   _____

6. Did Jack find the bug?

   _____

   -

The Lost Kitten

A little, gray kitten was lost.

It was lost in the grass.

The kitten was sad.

A little girl saw the kitten.

She took the kitten home.

1. What was lost?

_____

- - - - - - - - - - - - - - - - - - -

_____

2. Where was it lost?

_____

- - - - - - - - - - - - - - - - - - -

_____

3. What color was the kitten?

_____

- - - - - - - - - - - - - - - - - - -

_____

4. Who saw the kitten?

_____

- - - - - - - - - - - - - - - - - - -

_____

5. How did the kitten feel?

_____

- - - - - - - - - - - - - - - - - - -

_____

6. What did the girl do with the kitten?

_____

- - - - - - - - - - - - - - - - - - -

_____

Pam's Birthday

It is Pam's birthday.

All her friends will come.

They will get horns and hats.

They will eat cake and ice cream.

Pam and her friends will have fun

at her party.

1. Who is having a birthday?

_____

- -

_____

2. Who will come to the party?

_____

- -

_____

3. What will her friends get?

_____

- -

_____

4. What will they eat?

_____

- -

_____

5. Who will have fun?

_____

- -

_____

6. Where will they have fun?

_____

- -

_____

The Turtle and the Bug

It was a bright afternoon.

A little turtle swam in the pond.

It swam very slowly.

The turtle saw a black bug.

The black bug jumped away.

1. What was the afternoon like?

   _____

   -

   _____

2. Is the turtle big or little?

   _____

   -

   _____

3. Where did the turtle swim?

   _____

   -

   _____

4. How did the turtle swim?

   _____

   -

   _____

5. What did the turtle see?

   _____

   -

   _____

6. What did the bug do?

   _____

   -

   _____

Name _____

Ben's Frog

Ben had a frog in a box.

The frog was little and green.

Ben found it in the park.

The frog was by a rock.

He gave it to his friend.

1. What did Ben have?

_____

_____

2. Where did Ben keep his frog?

_____

_____

3. What color was the frog?

_____

_____

4. Where did Ben find the frog?

_____

_____

5. What was by a rock ?

_____

_____

6. What did Ben do with the frog?

_____

_____

The Frog

The little frog sat in the pond.

The frog sat very still.

A little bug flew by.

The frog jumped up and ate the bug.

Then the frog swam away.

1. Where did the frog sit?

_____

- -

_____

2. Was the frog big or little?

_____

- -

_____

3. How did the frog sit?

_____

- -

_____

4. What flew by?

_____

- -

_____

5. What did the frog do when it saw the bug?

_____

- -

_____

6. What did the frog do then?

_____

- -

_____

Jan and the Bug

Jan saw something on a flower.

It was a little, red bug.

The bug did not fly away.

It walked on Jan's hand.

Jan was happy with her new pet.

1. What did Jan see?

   _____

   _ _ _ _ _ _ _ _ _ _ _ _ _ _ _ _ _ _ _

   _____

2. Where did Jan see the bug?

   _____

   _ _ _ _ _ _ _ _ _ _ _ _ _ _ _ _ _ _ _

   _____

3. What color was the bug?

   _____

   _ _ _ _ _ _ _ _ _ _ _ _ _ _ _ _ _ _ _

   _____

4. Did the bug fly away?

   _____

   _ _ _ _ _ _ _ _ _ _ _ _ _ _ _ _ _ _ _

   _____

5. Where did the bug walk?

   _____

   _ _ _ _ _ _ _ _ _ _ _ _ _ _ _ _ _ _ _

   _____

6. Was Jan happy with her new pet?

   _____

   _ _ _ _ _ _ _ _ _ _ _ _ _ _ _ _ _ _ _

   _____

The Squirrel

The little, brown squirrel ran.

It saw a bag in the grass.

The squirrel looked into the bag.

It found a little peanut.

The squirrel ate the peanut.

1. What ran?

2. What did the squirrel look like?

3. What was in the grass?

4. Where did the squirrel look?

5. What did the squirrel find?

6. What did the squirrel do with the peanut?

The Lost Airplane

Ted ran up the hill.

He ran after a toy airplane.

The airplane flew into a tree.

Ted could not get the plane down.

He will have to get help.

I. Where did Ted run?

_____

- -

_____

2. What did Ted run after?

_____

- -

_____

3. What kind of airplane was it?

_____

- -

_____

4. Where did the plane go?

_____

- -

_____

5. Did Ted get the plane?

_____

- -

_____

6. What will Ted do?

_____

- -

_____

The Mouse

The little, gray mouse walked very softly.

The mouse sniffed.

It could smell something good.

It saw a little cookie.

The mouse ate the cookie.

1. How did the mouse walk?

_____

_____

2. What sniffed?

_____

_____

3. What color was the mouse?

_____

_____

4. What did the mouse smell?

_____

_____

5. What did the mouse see?

_____

_____

6. What did the mouse do?

_____

_____

FS-32043 Reading

The Clown

Come and see Pat's father in the circus.

Pat's dad is a funny clown.

Sometimes he rides a car.

Sometimes a seal rides with him.

Children laugh and clap.

1. Who can you come to see?

_____

- -

_____

2. Where can you see Pat's father?

_____

- -

_____

3. What does Pat's father do?

_____

- -

_____

4. What does he ride?

_____

- -

_____

5. What rides with Pat's father sometimes?

_____

- -

_____

6. What will the children do?

_____

- -

_____

The Bird

My friend has a pet bird.

It is a pretty, green bird.

It likes to eat seeds.

It can talk and sing.

Sometimes it just makes a lot of noise.

1. What does my friend have?

_____

- -

_____

2. What does the bird look like?

_____

- -

_____

3. What does the bird eat?

_____

- -

_____

4. What can the bird do?

_____

- -

_____

5. Do you think the bird can dance?

_____

- -

_____

6. What does it do sometimes?

_____

- -

_____

Tom's Box

Tom got a big, brown box.

He got it from his father.

Tom wants to make a clubhouse.

Tom will paint and fix it.

His friends will like it.

1. What did Tom get?

_____

- -

_____

2. What did the box look like?

_____

- -

_____

3. Where did he get the box?

_____

- -

_____

4. What does Tom want to make?

_____

- -

_____

5. What will Tom do with the box?

_____

- -

_____

6. Who will like the clubhouse?

_____

- -

_____

The Little Pig

Farmer Green has a pet pig.
It is little and white with a curly tail.
The pig likes to roll in the mud.
When the pig gets muddy,
Farmer Green gives it a bath.

1. Who has a pet pig?

_____

- - - - - - - - - - - - - - - - - -

_____

2. What does the pig look like?

_____

- - - - - - - - - - - - - - - - - -

_____

3. What kind of tail does it have?

_____

- - - - - - - - - - - - - - - - - -

_____

4. What does the pig like to do?

_____

- - - - - - - - - - - - - - - - - -

_____

5. When does Farmer Green give his pig a bath?

_____

- - - - - - - - - - - - - - - - - -

_____

6. Do you think the pig will like a bath?

_____

- - - - - - - - - - - - - - - - - -

_____

Linda's Mask

Linda went to the store.

She wanted to get a funny mask.

She got a mask with a big, red nose.

She wanted to surprise

Mom and Dad.

Mom and Dad laughed.

1. Where did Linda go?

_____

_____

2. What did she want to get?

_____

_____

3. What mask did Linda get?

_____

_____

4. What kind of nose did the mask have?

_____

_____

5. Who did Linda want to surprise?

_____

_____

6. What did Mom and Dad do?

_____

_____

Jake

Jake is a little, brown monkey.
Jake has on a red hat and coat.
Jake lives in the circus.
Give him a penny and he will
dance for you.

1. Who is Jake?

_____

_____

2. What color is Jake?

_____

_____

3. What does Jake have on?

_____

_____

4. Where does Jake live?

_____

_____

5. What can you give Jake?

_____

_____

6. What will Jake do for you?

_____

_____

Rain

Mike was playing ball in the yard.
Something wet fell on his head.
Mike looked up and saw dark clouds.
It began to rain and Mike got wet.
He ran into the house.

1. Where was Mike?

   _____

   _ _ _ _ _ _ _ _ _ _ _ _ _ _ _ _ _ _

   _____

2. What was Mike doing?

   _____

   _ _ _ _ _ _ _ _ _ _ _ _ _ _ _ _ _ _

   _____

3. What fell on his head?

   _____

   _ _ _ _ _ _ _ _ _ _ _ _ _ _ _ _ _ _

   _____

4. What did Mike see?

   _____

   _ _ _ _ _ _ _ _ _ _ _ _ _ _ _ _ _ _

   _____

5. Why did Mike get wet?

   _____

   _ _ _ _ _ _ _ _ _ _ _ _ _ _ _ _ _ _

   _____

6. Where did Mike go?

   _____

   _ _ _ _ _ _ _ _ _ _ _ _ _ _ _ _ _ _

   _____

The Owl and the Mouse

It was night.

A little, gray mouse was running.

A big owl was after it.

The mouse hid in the grass.

The owl did not get the mouse.

1. Was it morning or night?

_____

_ _

_____

2. What was running?

_____

_ _

_____

3. What was after the mouse?

_____

_ _

_____

4. Where did the mouse hide?

_____

_ _

_____

5. What color was the mouse?

_____

_ _

_____

6. Did the owl get the mouse?

_____

_ _

Lisa's New Pet

Lisa found a little, brown puppy.

She took it home and gave it a bath.

She gave the puppy good food
to eat.

The puppy did not have a home.

Lisa will keep the puppy.

1. What did Lisa find?

_____

_____

2. What color was the puppy?

_____

_____

3. Did the puppy have a home?

_____

_____

4. Where did Lisa take the puppy?

_____

_____

5. What is one thing Lisa did for the puppy?

_____

_____

_____

6. Do you think Lisa was good to the puppy?

_____

_____

Frank

Frank goes to the library every Monday.

Frank likes to read books.

He likes books about dinosaurs.

Frank reads books to

his little brother.

His brother likes to hear Frank read.

1. Where does Frank go?

_____

_ _ _ _ _ _ _ _ _ _ _ _ _ _ _ _ _ _ _ _

2. When does he go to the library?

_____

_ _ _ _ _ _ _ _ _ _ _ _ _ _ _ _ _ _ _ _

3. What books does he like?

_____

_ _ _ _ _ _ _ _ _ _ _ _ _ _ _ _ _ _ _ _

4. To whom does Frank read?

_____

_ _ _ _ _ _ _ _ _ _ _ _ _ _ _ _ _ _ _ _

5. Is Frank's brother big or little?

_____

_ _ _ _ _ _ _ _ _ _ _ _ _ _ _ _ _ _ _ _

6. Does Frank's brother like to hear him read?

_____

_ _ _ _ _ _ _ _ _ _ _ _ _ _ _ _ _ _ _ _

Name _____

Manfred the Show Dog

Mr. King has a show dog named Manfred.
He is a large white hound.
Manfred can stand very still.
Mr. King was happy.
Manfred won a ribbon.

1. What does Mr. King have?

   _____

2. What is the dog's name?

   _____

3. What color is the dog?

   _____

4. What kind of dog is he?

   _____

5. How does Manfred stand?

   _____

6. Who was happy?

   _____

7. What did Manfred win?

   _____

       FS-32043 Reading

Name _____

The Rocket

Joan and John built a rocket.
Joan's mother helped them.
They were very careful.
They made everything safe.
The rocket went very fast.

1. What is the boy's name?

_____

_____

2. What is the girl's name?

_____

3. What did the children build?

_____

_____

4. Who helped them?

_____

5. Who was careful?

_____

_____

6. What did they make safe?

_____

_____

7. How did the rocket go?

_____

_____

The Race

Mike and Mary ran a race at school.
They ran two miles.
It rained and rained the day of the race.
The track became muddy.
Mike and Mary finished the race anyway.

1. What is the name of the boy?

_____

_____

2. What is the name of the girl?

_____

_____

3. Where was the race?

_____

_____

4. How far did they run?

_____

_____

5. What happened the day of the race?

_____

_____

6. What happened to the track?

_____

_____

7. Who finished the race?

_____

_____

Name _____

Summer Camp

This summer José went to camp.
The camp is in the mountains.
There is a swimming pool at the camp.
Once a week the campers go horseback riding.
José liked camp very much.

1. Who is the story about?

   _____

   _____

2. Where did José go?

   _____

   _____

3. When did he go?

   _____

   _____

4. Where is the camp?

   _____

   _____

5. What do the children swim in?

   _____

   _____

6. Where do they go once a week?

   _____

   _____

7. How did José feel about camp?

   _____

   _____

Making Breakfast

On Sundays I make breakfast for my family.
First I cut apples and oranges.
Then I scramble eggs.
I also make pancakes with honey.
Next Sunday I'll make rolls.

1. What day do I make breakfast?

_____

_____

2. Who eats the breakfast?

_____

_____

3. What two things do I cut up?

_____

_____

4. What do I scramble?

_____

_____

5. What goes with the pancakes?

_____

_____

6. When will I make breakfast next?

_____

_____

7. What will I make next week?

_____

_____

Playing Tennis

Joe learned to play tennis.
He took eight lessons.
He learned to hit the ball over the net.
His father bought him new tennis shoes.
The shoes are green and white.

1. What is the boy's name?

_____

_____

2. What did he learn?

_____

_____

3. How many lessons did he take?

_____

_____

4. Where did he learn to hit the ball?

_____

_____

5. Who bought him shoes?

_____

_____

6. Were the shoes new or old?

_____

_____

7. What colors are the shoes?

_____

_____

Name _____

Across the Sea

We saw a film in school yesterday.
It was about two men who sailed across the sea.
They sailed on a raft.
They ate what they found in the water.
We thought they were brave men.

1. What did we see in school?

_____

_____

2. When did we see it?

_____

_____

3. How many men sailed?

_____

_____

4. Where did they sail?

_____

_____

5. What did they sail on?

_____

_____

6. What did they eat?

_____

_____

7. What did we think about the men?

_____

_____

Name _____

Our Team

Our baseball team won ten games.
We lost five games.
The coach says we had a good year.
The team is going to have a party on Saturday.
We will give the coach a gold cup.

1. What kind of team do we have?

   _____

   _____

2. How many games have we won?

   _____

   _____

3. How many games have we lost?

   _____

   _____

4. Who said we had a good year?

   _____

   _____

5. What is the team going to have?

   _____

   _____

6. What day is the party?

   _____

   _____

7. What will we give the coach?

   _____

   _____

FS-32043 Reading

The Space Museum

Our teacher took us to the space museum.
We looked at the stars and planets.
We saw a film on the planets.
We found out planets are different colors.
The planets and stars are very far away.
Someday people might visit the planets.

1. Who took us to the museum?

   -

2. What kind of museum was it?

   -

3. What did we see?

   -

4. What was the film about?

   -

5. How are the planets different?

   -

6. Are planets and stars close or far away?

   -

7. What might happen someday?

   -

Name _____

The Gold Watch

My grandfather gave me a pocket watch.
It is made of gold.
The watch has a long chain.
A long time ago the watch belonged to my great-grandfather.
That watch is very old!
But it is still running.

1. Who gave me the watch?

   ----

2. What kind of watch is it?

   ----

3. What is the watch made of?

   ----

4. What does the watch have?

   ----

5. Who did the watch belong to a long time ago?

   ----

6. Is the watch new or old?

   ----

7. What is the watch still doing?

FS-32043 Reading

Name _____

Tom Turtle

Terry has a pet turtle.
His name is Tom.
Tom lives in the yard.
One day Terry lost Tom.
Tom was lost for three weeks.
She found him in the flowers.

1. Who has a pet?

- -

_____

2. What is the pet?

- -

_____

3. What is the pet's name?

- -

_____

4. Where does Tom live?

- -

_____

5. What happened one day?

- -

_____

6. Where did Terry find Tom?

- -

_____

7. How many weeks was Tom lost?

- -

FS-32043 Reading

Name _____

The River

Bruce lives by the river.
The river is very big.
Ships go up the river.
Barges come down the river.
One day two ships crashed.
Now there is a hole in one.

1. What is the title of this story?

_____

_____

2. Who lives by the river?

_____

_____

3. Is the river big or small?

_____

_____

4. What goes up the river?

_____

_____

5. What comes down the river?

_____

_____

6. What happened one day?

_____

_____

7. What happened to one ship?

_____

_____

Zoos

Zoos have large and small animals.
The birds fly in cages.
The monkeys swing on bars.
The bears have caves.
The snakes are behind glass.
The animals are fed every day.

1. What is the name of this story?

_____

_____

2. What sizes are the animals in zoos?

_____

_____

3. Where do the birds fly?

_____

_____

4. On what do monkeys swing?

_____

_____

5. What do the bears have?

_____

_____

6. What are the snakes behind?

_____

_____

7. When are the animals fed?

_____

_____

Name _____

Bedtime

My bedtime is at 9 o'clock.
I go to my room at 8 o'clock.
First I read for ten minutes.
Then I brush my teeth.
After that I take a bath.
The last thing I do is put my clothes on the chair.

1. When is my bedtime?

_____

2. Where do I go?

_____

3. What time do I go?

_____

4. How long do I read?

_____

5. What do I do after I read?

_____

6. Do I take a bath or shower?

_____

7. What is the last thing I do?

_____

FS-32043 Reading

Name _____

Ice Skating

Joan likes to ice-skate.
She skates at a big rink.
She skates on Fridays.
Her friend Connie skates with her.
Connie wears a short skirt.
Joan wears white skates.

1. What does Joan like to do?

- -
_____

2. Where does she skate?

- -
_____

3. When does she skate?

- -
_____

4. Who is her friend?

- -
_____

5. Who skates with Joan?

- -
_____

6. What does Connie wear?

- -
_____

7. What does Joan wear?

- -

FS-32043 Reading

Kim's Mother

Kim's mother is a carpenter.

One day she came to school.

She showed the children how to hammer and nail.

The children worked for two hours.

She left at noon.

After lunch the children made wood boxes.

1. Who is a carpenter?

_____

_____

2. Where did she come one day?

_____

_____

3. What did she show the children?

_____

_____

4. How long did the children work?

_____

_____

5. When did she leave?

_____

_____

6. What did the children make?

_____

_____

7. When did they make them?

_____

_____

Bob's Party

Bob had a birthday party.
He took ten friends to the beach.
He brought along his dog.
The dog's name is Sid.
Sid ate all the hot dogs.
So ... lunch was rolls and cake!

1. Who had a party?

_____

_____

2. What kind of party was it?

_____

_____

3. How many friends did Bob bring?

_____

_____

4. Where did they go?

_____

_____

5. Who is Sid?

_____

_____

6. Who ate the hot dogs?

_____

_____

7. What was lunch?

_____

_____

Our New Car

Our family has a new car.
It is silver and black.
The seats have gray stripes.
There are seat belts in the front and back.
We call our new car the Silver Star.
It goes very fast.

1. What is the title of the story?

_____

_____

2. Who has a new car?

_____

_____

3. What colors are on the car?

_____

_____

4. What color are the stripes on the seats?

_____

_____

5. Where are the seat belts?

_____

_____

6. What is the name of the car?

_____

_____

7. Is the car fast or slow?

_____

_____

Name _____

The Snowmobile

In the winter we ride a snowmobile.
It is on our farm.
We live where it is very cold.
It is hard to drive a car in the snow.
The snowmobile goes fast.
The snowmobile is easy to drive.

1. What do we ride?

_____

_____

2. When do we ride it?

_____

_____

3. Where is the snowmobile?

_____

_____

4. Do we live where it is cold or hot?

_____

_____

5. What is hard to drive in the snow?

_____

_____

6. What goes fast?

_____

_____

7. What is easy to drive?

_____

_____

Name _____

Rain, Rain, Rain

It's raining outside. No sun, only clouds . . . no boys and girls playing . . . . , just rain, rain, rain. But . . . when it stops raining, I'll jump in puddles, play in the mud, and float paper boats in the street.

1. What is going on outside?

_____

2. Is the sun out?

_____

3. Are there clouds?

_____

4. Where are the boys and girls?

_____

5. What will I do with paper when it stops raining?

_____

6. Make a picture of the first sentence.

     FS-32043 Reading

Name _____

Monsters

I am reading such a good book. It is about monsters. These monsters are very nice. They play baseball, eat ice-cream and go to school. These monsters even have brothers and sisters. Monsters only live in books, you know. Let's keep it that way!

1. Who is this story about?

_____

2. Are they good or bad?

_____

3. Name three things that monsters do.

_____

4. Where is the only place that monsters live?

_____

5. Make a picture of the fourth sentence.

FS-32043 Reading

Name _____

A Mouse In Our House

There's a mouse in our house. We can't find it. We have never seen it. It eats our cheese. It makes noise at night. It makes our cat run all over the house. I hear it under my bed at night. Some day I'll see that mouse. Until then, I'll call it — Mr. Invisible!

1. Who is this story about?

_____

2. Where does the mouse live?

_____

3. What does it eat?

_____

Squeak!

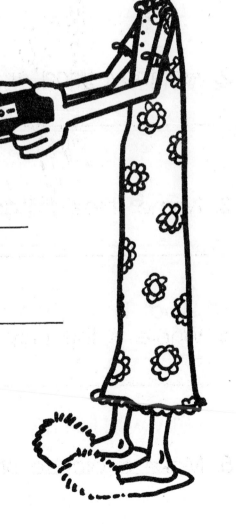

4. What does the cat do?

_____

5. Where can I hear the mouse at night?

_____

6. What is the mouse's name?

_____

7. Make a picture of the first sentence.

77

The Chocolate Cake Mess

Oh, Oh ....! Now I did it! I put my fingers in Mother's chocolate cake. She will be mad! What will I do now? Hide in my room? No! Throw the cake away? No! Tell my mom I goofed? Right! O.K. I'll lick my fingers and go find my mother.

1. What's the problem?

_____

2. Who will be mad?

_____

3. Name two wrong things I could do.

_____

4. What is the right thing to do?

_____

5. Why will I lick my fingers?

_____

Name _____

Baby-sitting

Did you ever baby-sit? Boy, it's hard work! You have to make sure the baby doesn't crawl out of the house. If he cries, you have to give him a bottle of milk. But baby-sitting is also fun. You can sure see a lot of T.V. And sometimes you can help yourself to snacks in the refrigerator.

1. What is this story about?

_____

2. Where could the baby crawl?

_____

3. Why can baby-sitting be fun?

_____

4. What do you do if the baby cries?

_____

5. Draw a picture of the last sentence.

FS-32043 Reading

Going to the Movies

My friend Jane and I go to the movies every Saturday. We always sit up front because you can see better. Jane buys popcorn and I help her eat it. Sometimes we see a Bugs Bunny cartoon. That's all folks!

1. Where do we go on Saturday?

_____

2. Why do we sit up front?

_____

3. How do I help Jane?

_____

4. What cartoon do we see?

_____

5. Make a picture of the first sentence.

FS-32043 Reading

Name _____

My Friend, Jimmy

It's nice to sit and talk to my friend. Jimmy and I tell jokes to each other. Sometimes he tells me about his monster dreams. I tell him about my pet turtle Speedy. We have learned a lot from each other.

1. Who do I talk to?

_____

2. What do we tell each other?

_____

3. What does Jimmy dream about?

_____

4. What is my pet called?

_____

5. Make a picture about this story.

FS-32043 Reading

Buying a Hamburger

It's fun to buy a hamburger. I stand in line. Then the man asks me what I want. I ask for a hamburger with cheese and ketchup on it. I also ask for french fries and a drink. Now what kind of a drink shall I have?

1. Why did I stand in line?

_____

2. What did I want on my hamburger?

_____

3. What kind of potatoes did I ask for?

_____

4. What kind of drink do you think I had?

_____

5. Make a picture about this story.

Name _____

What Does It Mean?

Some words have the same meaning. Father and Dad . . . fast and speedy . . . sleep and snooze . . . tender and soft . . . big and large.

...Or call me Pop!

1. What word means the same as Father?

_____

2. What word means the same as soft?

_____

3. What word means the same as speedy?

_____

4. What word means the same as sleep?

_____

5. What word means the same as big?

_____

6. Name two other words that mean the same.

_____

FS-32043 Reading

My Bicycle

My bicycle is super. It is ten-speed and painted red. It can go so fast. I like to take long trips with my bicycle. Sometimes I honk my horn when I ride past my friend's house. I can do a trick. Sometimes I ride without my hands on the handlebars. When I go to sleep, I keep my bike next to my bed. Goodnight!

Let's go!

1. What is this story about?

_____

2. What color is my bike?

_____

3. What does my friend hear when I go by?

_____

4. Name a trick I can do.

_____

5. Where is my bike when I go to bed?

_____

FS-32043 Reading

Name _____

Read the story.

That bird cannot fly. It has a hurt wing. I will take care of it. Then the bird will get well.

Read the sentences below. Cut them out and paste them in the right order.

1	
2	
3	
4	

Cut.

One wing is hurt.

I will help the bird.

The bird will get well.

It cannot fly.

FS-32043 Reading

Read the story.

Mike looked at his bike. "Oh no, I have a flat tire," he said. "I will fix it now. Then I will pump up the tire."

Read the sentences below. Cut them out and paste them in the right order.

1	
2	
3	
4	

Cut.

He will fix it.

Mike saw the flat tire.

Mike will pump air in the tire.

"Oh no, I have a flat tire."

Name _____

Read the story.

Nan hears a bell. She runs to get her money. Now she sees the red truck. She wants to buy ice cream.

Read the sentences below. Cut them out and paste them in the right order.

1	
2	
3	
4	

Cut.

Nan gets her money.

She can see the red truck.

The bell is ringing.

Nan will buy ice cream.

FS-32043 Reading

Name _____

Read the story.

Watch me mix a new color! First I will put some white paint in the dish. Now I will add red paint. I made pink paint.

Read the sentences below. Cut them out and paste them in the right order.

1	
2	
3	
4	

Cut.

I will add red paint.

Look at the new color.

I will put white paint in the dish.

Watch me mix a new color!

FS-32043 Reading

Name _____

Read the story.

I need to phone my mother. May I use your phone? I will tell Mother where I am. Then I'll ask if I may play.

Read the sentences below. Cut them out and paste them in the right order.

1	
2	
3	
4	

Cut.

I will tell Mom where I am.

I'll ask Mother if I may play.

I must make a phone call.

May I use your phone?

FS-32043 Reading

Name _____

Read the story.

"I can trace that," said Pam. "Put the shape on the paper. Now I will trace around it. Then I can cut it out."

Read the sentences below. Cut them out and paste them in the right order.

1	
2	
3	
4	

Cut.

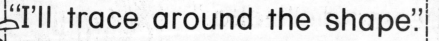

"I'll trace around the shape."

Pam said, "I can trace."

"Now I will cut it out."

"Put the shape on the paper."

Name _____

Read the story.

It is the first day of school. I found my new room. The teacher said, "Hello. I'm Miss Rand." Then I sat at my desk.

Read the sentences below. Cut them out and paste them in the right order.

1	
2	
3	
4	

Cut.

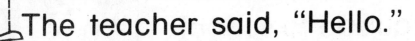
The teacher said, "Hello."

I found my desk.

It is the first day of school.

I found my class.

FS-32043 Reading

Name _____

Read the story.

    Don said, "I'm riding my bike today." He rode down the street. He saw Pat on his bike. They rode to school.

Read the sentences below. Cut them out and paste them in the right order.

1	
2	
3	
4	

Cut.

Pat and Don rode to school.

Don saw Pat.

Don rode down the street.

"I'm riding my bike," said Don.

FS-32043 Reading

Name _____

Read the story.

Kim told Mother to look outside. The sky is getting dark. Now the wind is blowing. It is starting to rain!

Read the sentences below. Cut them out and paste them in the right order.

1	
2	
3	
4	

Cut.

The wind is blowing.

Kim told Mother to look.

It is raining now.

The sky is getting dark.

FS-32043 Reading

Name _____

Read the story.

I like to play soccer. My friend Ted is on my team. After school we will go to our game. Then Ted's dad will take us home.

Read the sentences below. Cut them out and paste them in the right order.

1	
2	
3	
4	

Cut.

My friend is on my team.

We will go to our game.

We will go home.

I like to play soccer.

FS-32043 Reading

Name _____

Read the story.

"It is time for your spelling test," said
Mr. Green. "Write your name on the paper.
Then write the numbers from one to ten. Now
spell the word 'cat'."

Read the sentences below. Cut them out and paste
them in the right order.

1	
2	
3	
4	
5	

Cut.

"Write your name."

"Spell the word 'cat'."

Mr. Green started to talk.

"Put numbers on your paper."

"It is time for the test."

Name _____

Read the story.

My fish are fun to watch. They hide in the grass. Then I drop in some food. They swim up to the top to eat. Then they hide in the grass again.

Read the sentences below. Cut them out and paste them in the right order.

1	
2	
3	
4	
5	

Cut.

I like to watch my fish.

I feed the fish.

The fish hide in the grass.

They eat and hide again.

They swim to the top.

Name _____

Read the story.

My dog sits by the door. I come home and he licks my hand. He barks and rolls over. He wants a treat. I always give him a treat after school.

Read the sentences below. Cut them out and paste them in the right order.

1	
2	
3	
4	
5	

Cut.

I give my dog a treat.

He barks and rolls over.

He licks my hand.

My dog sits at the door.

I come home from school.

FS-32043 Reading

Name _____

Read the story.

Today is my little sister's birthday. My mother is baking a cake. Then she will frost the cake. I will put three candles on the cake. Then we will sing "Happy Birthday".

Read the sentences below. Cut them out and paste them in the right order.

1	
2	
3	
4	
5	

Cut.

She will frost the cake.

We will sing to my sister.

Mother will bake a cake.

I will put on the candles.

Today is my sister's birthday.

FS-32043 Reading

Name _____

Read the story.

Run home from school. Ask your mother if you can come to my house. Then ride over on your bike. We will ride bikes. Then we can play a game.

Read the sentences below. Cut them out and paste them in the right order.

1	
2	
3	
4	
5	

Cut.

We will ride bikes.

You must ask your mother.

We will play a game.

Ride your bike to my house.

Run home from school.

FS-32043 Reading

Name _____

Read the story.

"You got a letter in the mail," said Mother. I was surprised. I opened the letter. It was about Tom's party. I will go to the party.

Read the sentences below. Cut them out and paste them in the right order.

1	
2	
3	
4	
5	

Cut.

I was surprised.

The letter is about a party.

Mother told me I got a letter.

I opened the letter.

I will go to the party.

FS-32043 Reading

Name _____

Read the story.

I need a book about cats. I will go to the library. Then I will find some books. I can take the books home with me. Daddy and I will read them.

Read the sentences below. Cut them out and paste them in the right order.

1	
2	
3	
4	
5	

Cut.

Daddy and I will read them.

I need a book.

I will find the books.

I will go to the library.

I will take the books home.

FS-32043 Reading

Name _____

Read the story.

Last June I planted my seeds. A long green vine grew. Orange flowers grew on the vine. Each flower will become a pumpkin. I can give pumpkins to my friends.

Read the sentences below. Cut them out and paste them in the right order.

1	
2	
3	
4	
5	

Cut.

A long green vine grew.

The flowers will be pumpkins.

I planted some seeds.

I will give pumpkins away.

Then orange flowers grew.

FS-32043 Reading

Name _____

Read the story.

I found a cat. It had a tag on its neck with a phone number. I called and a man came to get the lost cat. He told me it was his boy's cat.

Read the sentences below. Cut them out and paste them in the right order.

1	
2	
3	
4	
5	

Cut.

I called the number.

He came to my house.

He took the cat.

I found a cat.

I talked to a man.

   FS-32043 Reading

Name _____

Read the story.

I got my pumpkin yesterday. I marked the eyes, nose and mouth. My sister will cut it. Then I will take the seeds out. I will put the jack-o-lantern in the window.

Read the sentences below. Cut them out and paste them in the right order.

1	
2	
3	
4	
5	

Cut.

I marked the face.

I will take the seeds out.

Now I have my pumpkin.

My jack-o-lantern is done.

My sister will help.

FS-32043 Reading

Answer Key

My Cat

My cat is black.
She likes to play.

1. __My__ cat is black.

2. My __cat__ is black.

3. My cat is __black__.

4. __She__ likes to play.

5. She likes to __play__.

6. My __cat__ is __black__.

   She __likes__ to __play__.

Page 1

School

I go to school.
School is fun.

1. __I__ go to school.

2. I __go__ to school.

3. I go to __school__

4. __School__ is fun.

5. School is __fun__.

6. __I__ __go__ to __school__

   School __is__ fun.

Page 2

Good morning.

Jane Jumps

Jane can jump.
She can jump ten times.

1. __Jane__ can jump.

2. Jane can __jump__

3. She __can__ jump ten times.

4. She can jump __ten__ times.

5. She can jump ten __times__

6. __Jane__ can __jump__

   She __can__ jump __ten__ times.

Page 3

Bugs

Pam likes bugs.
She likes red bugs.

For lunch!

1. __Pam__ likes bugs.

2. Pam __likes__ bugs.

3. Pam likes __bugs__

4. __She__ likes red bugs.

5. She likes __red__ bugs.

6. __Pam__ likes __bugs__

   She __likes__ red __bugs__

Page 4

105

FS-32043 Reading

Answer Key

Tom's Dog

Tom has a big dog.
The dog sleeps with Tom.

Arf! Arf!

1. __Tom__ has a big dog.

2. Tom has a __big__ dog.

3. Tom has a big __dog__

4. The dog __sleeps__ with Tom.

5. The dog sleeps __with__ Tom.

6. __Tom__ has __a__ big __dog__

   The __dog__ sleeps __with__ Tom.

Name

Jets

Jets are planes.
They go very fast.

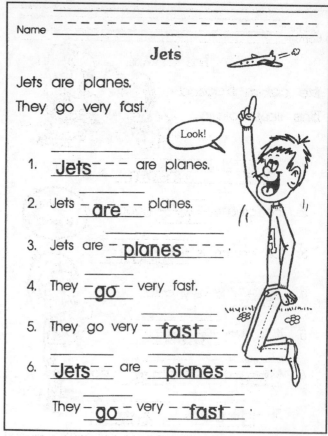

Look!

1. __Jets__ are planes.

2. Jets __are__ planes.

3. Jets are __planes__ .

4. They __go__ very fast.

5. They go very __fast__

6. __Jets__ are __planes__

   They __go__ very __fast__

Name

The Ball

Jim has a ball.
It is yellow and red.

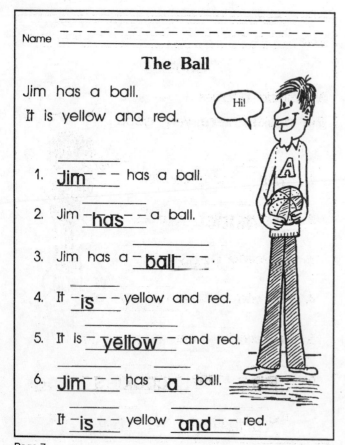

Hi!

1. __Jim__ has a ball.

2. Jim __has__ a ball.

3. Jim has a __ball__ .

4. It __is__ yellow and red.

5. It is __yellow__ and red.

6. __Jim__ has __a__ ball.

   It __is__ yellow __and__ red.

Name

Balloons

Ted has three balloons.
The balloons are red.

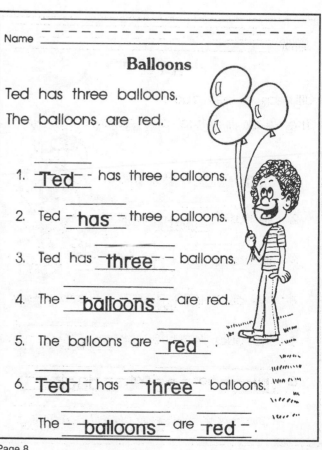

1. __Ted__ has three balloons.

2. Ted __has__ three balloons.

3. Ted has __three__ balloons.

4. The __balloons__ are red.

5. The balloons are __red__ .

6. __Ted__ has __three__ balloons.

   The __balloons__ are __red__ .

106

Answer Key

Ice Cream

Ice cream is good.
It is very cold.

Oh, this is good!

1. __Ice__ __cream__ is good.

2. Ice cream __is__ good.

3. Ice cream is __good__

4. __It__ is very cold.

5. It is very __cold__

6. __Ice__ cream __is__ good.

It __is__ very __cold__.

The Train

Nan has a toy train.
She plays with it every day.

I like my doll too!

1. __Nan__ has a toy train.

2. Nan has a __toy__ train.

3. Nan has a toy __train__

4. She __plays__ with it every day.

5. She plays with it __every__ day.

6. __Nan__ has __a__ toy __train__.

She __plays__ with __it__ every __day__

A Pet

Jill has a pet duck.
The duck is white and yellow.

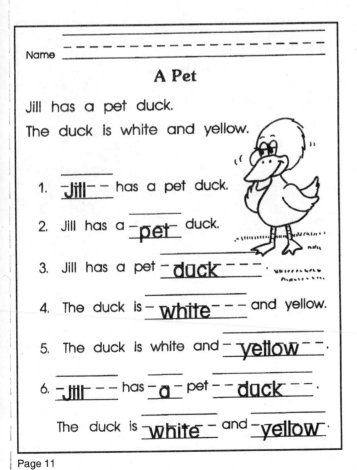

1. __Jill__ has a pet duck.

2. Jill has a __pet__ duck.

3. Jill has a pet __duck__

4. The duck is __white__ and yellow.

5. The duck is white and __yellow__

6. __Jill__ has __a__ pet __duck__

The duck is __white__ and __yellow__

Cookies

Bill made cookies.
The cookies were very good.

Yum!

Chomp!

1. __Bill__ made cookies.

2. Bill __made__ cookies.

3. Bill made __cookies__

4. The cookies were __very__ good.

5. The cookies were very __good__

6. __Bill__ made __cookies__

The __cookies__ were __very__ good.

Answer Key

Name

Books

I like books.
Books are fun for me.

I love to read!

1. <u>I</u> like books.

2. I <u>like</u> books.

3. I like <u>books</u>.

4. <u>Books</u> are fun for <u>me</u>.

5. Books <u>are</u> fun <u>for</u> me.

6. I <u>like</u> books.

<u>Books</u> are <u>fun</u> for <u>me</u>.

Page 13

Name

A Plant

Jane has a plant.
It is green.

I like my plant.

1. <u>Jane</u> has a plant.

2. Jane <u>has</u> a plant.

3. Jane has a <u>plant</u>.

4. <u>It</u> is green.

5. It is <u>green</u>.

6. <u>Jane</u> has <u>a</u> plant.

<u>It</u> is <u>green</u>.

Page 14

Name

Hide and Seek

Dan and Mary play hide and seek.
They hide in the room.

1. Dan and <u>Mary</u> play hide and seek.

2. Dan and Mary <u>play</u> hide and seek.

3. Dan and Mary play <u>hide</u> and seek.

4. They hide <u>in</u> the room.

5. They hide in the <u>room</u>.

6. Dan <u>and</u> Mary <u>play</u> hide <u>and</u> seek.

<u>They</u> hide <u>in</u> the <u>room</u>.

Page 15

Name

My Boat

I have a little boat.
I float it in the water.

1. I <u>have</u> a little boat.

2. I have a <u>little</u> boat.

3. I have a <u>little</u> <u>boat</u>.

4. I <u>float</u> it in the water.

5. I float it in the <u>water</u>.

6. I <u>have</u> a <u>little</u> boat.

<u>I</u> float <u>it</u> in <u>the</u> water.

Page 16

108

Answer Key

The Green Car

I saw a little green car.
It went up the street.

1. I _saw_ a little green car.

2. I saw a _little_ green _car_.

3. It _went_ up the _street_.

4. It went _up_ the street.

5. It went up _the_ street.

6. I _saw_ a _little_ green _car_.

   It _went_ up _the_ street.

Page 17

The Doll

Tim has a doll.
It is his very best friend.

1. _Tim_ has a doll.

2. Tim _has_ a doll.

3. Tim has a _doll_.

4. It is _his_ very best friend.

5. It is his _very_ best _friend_.

6. _Tim_ has _a_ doll.

   _It_ is _his_ very _best_ friend.

Page 18

Colors

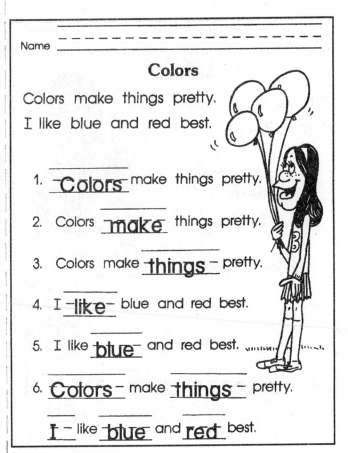

Colors make things pretty.
I like blue and red best.

1. _Colors_ make things pretty.

2. Colors _make_ things pretty.

3. Colors make _things_ pretty.

4. I _like_ blue and red best.

5. I like _blue_ and red best.

6. _Colors_ make _things_ pretty.

   _I_ like _blue_ and _red_ best.

Page 19

My Monster

My monster has a big blue hat.
The hat has a rose on it.

1. What does my monster have?

Your monster has a hat.

2. Is it big or little?

It is big.

3. What color is the hat?

The hat is blue.

4. Does the hat have a cat on it?

No, the hat does not have a cat on it.

5. What does the hat have on it?

The hat has a rose on it.

Page 20

109

FS-32043 Reading

Answer Key

Name _____

Seeds

I planted four seeds.
Now they are big green plants.

1. What did I plant?

You planted seeds.

2. How many did I plant?

You planted four.

3. Are the plants big?

Yes, the plants are big.

4. Are the plants red?

No, the plants are not red.

5. What color are the plants?

The plants are green.

Page 21

Name _____

Blocks

Jim plays with big blocks.
He does not make boats.
He just makes trains and trucks.

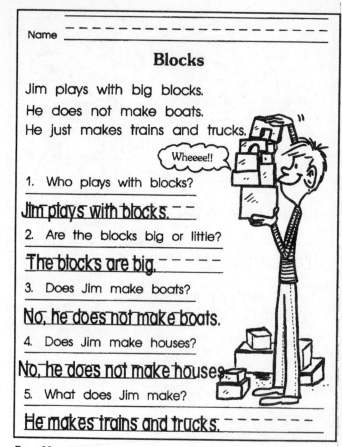

Wheeee!!

1. Who plays with blocks?

Jim plays with blocks.

2. Are the blocks big or little?

The blocks are big.

3. Does Jim make boats?

No, he does not make boats.

4. Does Jim make houses?

No, he does not make houses.

5. What does Jim make?

He makes trains and trucks.

Page 22

Name _____

Mice

Jane saw some mice.
They were gray.
They ate cheese and cookies.

They were so cute!

1. What did Jane see?

Jane saw mice.

2. Were the mice white?

No, they were not white.

3. Were the mice gray?

Yes, they were gray.

4. Did the mice eat cheese?

Yes, they ate cheese.

5. Did the mice eat cookies?

Yes, they ate cookies.

Page 23

Name _____

The Monkey

The monkey has fun.
He plays all day.
He is in the zoo.

munch
munch

1. Who is the story about?

The story is about a monkey.

2. Does the monkey have fun?

Yes, the monkey has fun.

3. Does the monkey play?

Yes, the monkey plays.

4. When does the monkey play?

He plays all day.

5. Where is the monkey?

He is in the zoo.

How cute!

Page 24

Answer Key

Name _____

The Elephant

The elephant is big and gray.

His trunk is long.

His ears are wide.

1. Who is the story about?

The story is about an elephant.

2. Is the elephant big or little?

The elephant is big.

3. What color is the elephant?

The elephant is gray.

4. What is long?

His trunk is long.

5. What is wide?

His ears are wide.

Page 25

Name _____

Bill's Bike

Bill has a new bike.
It has two wheels.
It is blue.

1. Who has a bike?

Bill has a bike.

2. Is the bike old or new?

The bike is new.

3. Does the bike have three wheels?

No, the bike does not have three wheels.

4. How many wheels does the bike have?

The bike has two wheels.

5. What color is the bike?

The bike is blue.

Page 26

Name _____

The Clown

A clown came to school.

She came on Monday.

She had six balloons.

1. Who came to school?

A clown came to school.

2. What day did she come?

She came on Monday.

3. Was the clown a boy?

No, the clown was not a boy.

4. How many balloons are there?

There are six balloons.

5. What did the clown have?

The clown had balloons.

Page 27

Name _____

Nan's Hamster

Nan has a brown hamster.

The hamster has a little wheel.

Nan loves her hamster.

1. Who has a hamster?

Nan has a hamster.

2. What color is the hamster?

It is brown.

3. Who has a wheel?

The hamster has a wheel.

4. Is the wheel big or little?

The wheel is little.

5. Who loves the hamster?

Nan loves the hamster.

Page 28

FS-32043 Reading

Answer Key

Name _____

Our Cat

Our brown cat ran away.
She came back after five days.
I was so glad!

1. What color is our cat?

Your cat is brown.

2. What did our cat do?

Your cat came back.

3. Did she come back after ten days?

No, she didn't come back after ten days.

4. Did she come back after four days?

No, she didn't come back after four days.

5. After how many days did she come back?

She came back after five days.

Page 29

Name _____

Sue's Snake

Sue has a pet snake.
It is in a green box.
The box has a top.

Guess what I have?

1. Who has a pet?

Sue has a pet.

2. What is the pet?

It is a snake.

3. Is the pet in a tree?

No, the pet is not in a tree.

4. What color is the box?

The box is green.

5. Does the box have a top?

Yes, the box has a top.

Page 30

Name _____

A Game

Bob and Bill played a ball game.

They played at the park.

They played on Saturday.

1. Who played with Bob?

Bill played with Bob.

2. What did they play?

They played ball.

3. Where did they play?

They played at the park.

4. Did they play on Monday?

No, they did not play on Monday.

5. When did they play?

They played on Saturday.

Page 31

Name _____

Joe's Lunch

Joe ate a red apple.
It was in his big lunch box.
Yum, yum!

I like apples!

1. Who ate something?

Joe ate something.

2. What color was it?

It was red.

3. What did Joe eat?

Joe ate an apple.

4. Was Joe's lunch box little?

No, Joe's lunch box was not little.

5. Was Joe's lunch box big?

Yes, Joe's lunch box was big.

Page 32

112

FS-32043 Reading

Answer Key

Name _____

The Park

John went to a park.
He played on the swings.
He jumped in the pool.
He did not go on the slide.

1. Is John a boy or a girl?

John is a boy.

2. Where did John go?

He went to a park.

3. Did he play on the slide?

No, he did not play on the slide.

4. What did he play on?

He played on the swings.

5. Where did he jump?

He jumped in the pool.

Page 33

Name _____

Skates

I have skates.
I skate every day.
I skate at school.
I skate at home.
I do not skate in the park.

whoopeeeee!

1. What do I have?

You have skates.

2. When do I skate?

You skate every day.

3. Do I skate at school?

Yes, you skate at school.

4. Do I skate in the park?

No, you don't skate in the park.

5. Do I skate at home?

Yes, you skate at home.

Page 34

Name _____

Peter Pig

Peter Pig lives on a farm.
He is pink.
He is fat.
He eats apples.

He is my best pig.

1. What is the pig's name?

His name is Peter Pig.

2. Where does he live?

He lives on a farm.

3. What color is he?

He is pink.

4. Is he fat or thin?

He is fat.

5. What does he eat?

He eats apples.

Page 35

Name _____   Skill: Reading comprehension

Jack's Bug

Jack ran in the park.
He ran after a lightning bug.
The little bug hid in the grass.
Jack looked and looked.
But he did not find it.

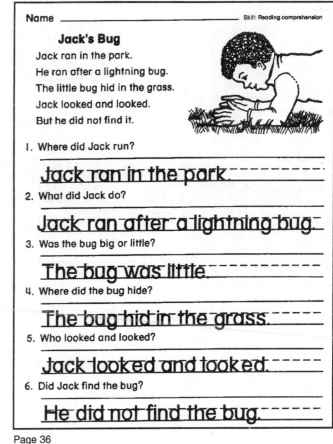

1. Where did Jack run?

Jack ran in the park.

2. What did Jack do?

Jack ran after a lightning bug.

3. Was the bug big or little?

The bug was little.

4. Where did the bug hide?

The bug hid in the grass.

5. Who looked and looked?

Jack looked and looked.

6. Did Jack find the bug?

He did not find the bug.

Page 36

FS-32043 Reading

Answer Key

The Lost Kitten

A little, gray kitten was lost.
It was lost in the grass.
The kitten was sad.
A little girl saw the kitten.
She took the kitten home.

1. What was lost?

A kitten was lost.

2. Where was it lost?

It was lost in the grass.

3. What color was the kitten?

The kitten was gray.

4. Who saw the kitten?

A little girl saw the kitten.

5. How did the kitten feel?

The kitten was sad.

6. What did the girl do with the kitten?

The girl took the kitten home.

Page 37

Pam's Birthday

It is Pam's birthday.
All her friends will come.
They will get horns and hats.
They will eat cake and ice cream.
Pam and her friends will have fun
at her party.

1. Who is having a birthday?

Pam is having a birthday.

2. Who will come to the party?

All her friends will come.

3. What will her friends get?

Her friends will get horns and hats.

4. What will they eat?

They will eat cake and ice cream.

5. Who will have fun?

Pam and her friends will have fun.

6. Where will they have fun?

They will have fun at her party.

Page 38

The Turtle and the Bug

It was a bright afternoon.
A little turtle swam in the pond.
It swam very slowly.
The turtle saw a black bug.
The black bug jumped away.

1. What was the afternoon like?

The afternoon was bright.

2. Is the turtle big or little?

The turtle is little.

3. Where did the turtle swim?

The turtle swam in the pond.

4. How did the turtle swim?

The turtle swam slowly.

5. What did the turtle see?

The turtle saw a black bug.

6. What did the bug do?

The bug jumped away.

Page 39

Ben's Frog

Ben had a frog in a box.
The frog was little and green.
Ben found it in the park.
The frog was by a rock.
He gave it to his friend.

1. What did Ben have?

Ben had a frog.

2. Where did Ben keep his frog?

Ben kept his frog in a box.

3. What color was the frog?

The frog was green.

4. Where did Ben find the frog?

Ben found the frog in the park.

5. What was by a rock ?

The frog was by a rock.

6. What did Ben do with the frog?

Ben gave the frog to his friend.

Page 40

Answer Key

Name _____

Skill: Reading comprehension

The Frog

The little frog sat in the pond.
The frog sat very still.
A little bug flew by.
The frog jumped up and ate the bug.
Then the frog swam away.

1. Where did the frog sit?

The frog sat in the pond.

2. Was the frog big or little?

The frog was little.

3. How did the frog sit?

The frog sat very still.

4. What flew by?

A little bug flew by.

5. What did the frog do when it saw the bug?

The frog jumped up and ate the bug.

6. What did the frog do then?

The frog swam away.

Page 41

Name _____

Skill: Reading comprehension

Jan and the Bug

Jan saw something on a flower.
It was a little, red bug.
The bug did not fly away.
It walked on Jan's hand.
Jan was happy with her new pet.

1. What did Jan see?

Jan saw a bug.

2. Where did Jan see the bug?

She saw it on a flower.

3. What color was the bug?

The bug was red.

4. Did the bug fly away?

No, the bug did not fly away.

5. Where did the bug walk?

The bug walked on Jan's hand.

6. Was Jan happy with her new pet?

Yes, Jan was happy with her new pet.

Page 42

Name _____

Skill: Reading comprehension

The Squirrel

The little, brown squirrel ran.
It saw a bag in the grass.
The squirrel looked into the bag.
It found a little peanut.
The squirrel ate the peanut.

1. What ran?

A squirrel ran.

2. What did the squirrel look like?

The squirrel was little and brown.

3. What was in the grass?

A bag was in the grass.

4. Where did the squirrel look?

The squirrel looked into the bag.

5. What did the squirrel find?

The squirrel found a little peanut.

6. What did the squirrel do with the peanut?

The squirrel ate the peanut.

Page 43

Name _____

Skill: Reading comprehension

The Lost Airplane

Ted ran up the hill.
He ran after a toy airplane.
The airplane flew into a tree.
Ted could not get the plane down.
He will have to get help.

1. Where did Ted run?

Ted ran up the hill.

2. What did Ted run after?

Ted ran after a toy airplane.

3. What kind of airplane was it?

It was a toy airplane.

4. Where did the plane go?

The plane flew into a tree.

5. Did Ted get the plane?

Ted could not get the plane.

6. What will Ted do?

Ted will get help.

Page 44

115

FS-32043 Reading

Answer Key

Name _____

Skill: Reading comprehension

The Mouse

The little, gray mouse walked very softly.
The mouse sniffed.
It could smell something good.
It saw a little cookie.
The mouse ate the cookie.

1. How did the mouse walk?

The mouse walked softly.

2. What sniffed?

The mouse sniffed.

3. What color was the mouse?

The mouse was gray.

4. What did the mouse smell?

The mouse smelled something good.

5. What did the mouse see?

The mouse saw a little cookie.

6. What did the mouse do?

The mouse ate the cookie.

Page 45

Name _____

Skill: Reading comprehension

The Clown

Come and see Pat's father in the circus.
Pat's dad is a funny clown.
Sometimes he rides a car.
Sometimes a seal rides with him.
Children laugh and clap.

1. Who can you come to see?

I can come to see Pat's father

2. Where can you see Pat's father?

I can see Pat's father in the circus.

3. What does Pat's father do?

He is a funny clown.

4. What does he ride?

He rides a car.

5. What rides with Pat's father sometimes?

Sometimes a seal rides with him.

6. What will the children do?

The children will laugh and clap.

Page 46

Name _____

Skill: Reading comprehension

The Bird

My friend has a pet bird.
It is a pretty, green bird.
It likes to eat seeds.
It can talk and sing.
Sometimes it just makes a lot of noise.

1. What does my friend have?

Your friend has a pet bird.

2. What does the bird look like?

The bird is pretty and green.

3. What does the bird eat?

The bird eats seeds.

4. What can the bird do?

The bird can talk and sing.

5. Do you think the bird can dance?

Answers will vary.

6. What does it do sometimes?

Sometimes it makes a lot of noise.

Page 47

Name _____

Skill: Reading comprehension

Tom's Box

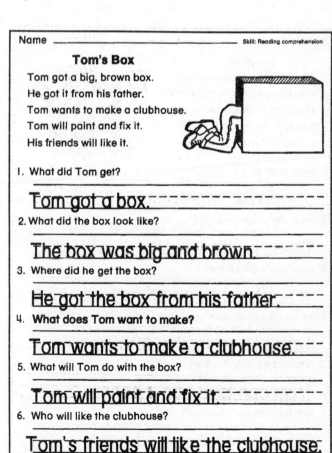

Tom got a big, brown box.
He got it from his father.
Tom wants to make a clubhouse.
Tom will paint and fix it.
His friends will like it.

1. What did Tom get?

Tom got a box.

2. What did the box look like?

The box was big and brown.

3. Where did he get the box?

He got the box from his father.

4. What does Tom want to make?

Tom wants to make a clubhouse.

5. What will Tom do with the box?

Tom will paint and fix it.

6. Who will like the clubhouse?

Tom's friends will like the clubhouse.

Page 48

FS-32043 Reading

Answer Key

Name _____

The Little Pig

Farmer Green has a pet pig.
It is little and white with a curly tail.
The pig likes to roll in the mud.
When the pig gets muddy,
Farmer Green gives it a bath.

1. Who has a pet pig?

   Farmer Green has a pet pig.

2. What does the pig look like?

   It is little and white.

3. What kind of tail does it have?

   It has a curly tail.

4. What does the pig like to do?

   The pig likes to roll in the mud.

5. When does Farmer Green give his pig a bath?

   Farmer Green gives his pig a bath when it is muddy.

6. Do you think the pig will like a bath?

   Answers will vary.

Page 49

Name _____

Linda's Mask

Linda went to the store.
She wanted to get a funny mask.
She got a mask with a big, red nose.
She wanted to surprise
Mom and Dad.
Mom and Dad laughed.

1. Where did Linda go?

   Linda went to the store.

2. What did she want to get?

   She wanted to get a funny mask.

3. What mask did Linda get?

   She got a mask with a big, red nose.

4. What kind of nose did the mask have?

   The mask had a big, red nose.

5. Who did Linda want to surprise?

   Linda wanted to surprise Mom and Dad.

6. What did Mom and Dad do?

   Mom and Dad laughed.

Page 50

Name _____

Jake

Jake is a little, brown monkey.
Jake has on a red hat and coat.
Jake lives in the circus.
Give him a penny and he will
dance for you.

1. Who is Jake?

   Jake is a monkey.

2. What color is Jake?

   Jake is brown.

3. What does Jake have on?

   Jake has on a red hat and coat.

4. Where does Jake live?

   Jake lives in the circus.

5. What can you give Jake?

   You can give him a penny.

6. What will Jake do for you?

   Jake will dance for you.

Page 51

Name _____

Rain

Mike was playing ball in the yard.
Something wet fell on his head.
Mike looked up and saw dark clouds.
It began to rain and Mike got wet.
He ran into the house.

1. Where was Mike?

   Mike was in the yard.

2. What was Mike doing?

   Mike was playing ball.

3. What fell on his head?

   Rain fell on his head.

4. What did Mike see?

   Mike saw dark clouds.

5. Why did Mike get wet?

   Mike got wet because it began to rain.

6. Where did Mike go?

   Mike ran into the house.

Page 52

117

Answer Key

Name

Skill: Reading comprehension

The Owl and the Mouse
It was night.
A little, gray mouse was running.
A big owl was after it.
The mouse hid in the grass.
The owl did not get the mouse.

1. Was it morning or night?

It was night.

2. What was running?

A little, gray mouse was running.

3. What was after the mouse?

A big owl was after the mouse.

4. Where did the mouse hide?

The mouse hid in the grass.

5. What color was the mouse?

The mouse was gray.

6. Did the owl get the mouse?

No, the owl did not get the mouse.

Page 53

Name

Skill: Reading comprehension

Lisa's New Pet
Lisa found a little, brown puppy.
She took it home and gave it a bath.
She gave the puppy good food
to eat.
The puppy did not have a home.
Lisa will keep the puppy.

1. What did Lisa find?

Lisa found a puppy.

2. What color was the puppy?

The puppy was brown.

3. Did the puppy have a home?

No, the puppy did not have a home.

4. Where did Lisa take the puppy?

Lisa took the puppy to her house.

5. What is one thing Lisa did for the puppy?

Lisa gave the puppy food/a bath.

6. Do you think Lisa was good to the puppy?

Answers will vary.

Page 54

Name

Skill: Reading comprehension

Frank
Frank goes to the library every Monday.
Frank likes to read books.
He likes books about dinosaurs.
Frank reads books to
his little brother.
His brother likes to hear Frank read.

1. Where does Frank go?

Frank goes to the library.

2. When does he go to the library?

He goes to the library every Monday.

3. What books does he like?

He likes books about dinosaurs.

4. To whom does Frank read?

Frank reads to his little brother.

5. Is Frank's brother big or little?

Frank's brother is little.

6. Does Frank's brother like to hear him read?

Yes, Frank's brother likes to hear him read.

Page 55

Name

Manfred the Show Dog
Mr. King has a show dog named Manfred.
He is a large white hound.
Manfred can stand very still.
Mr. King was happy.
Manfred won a ribbon.

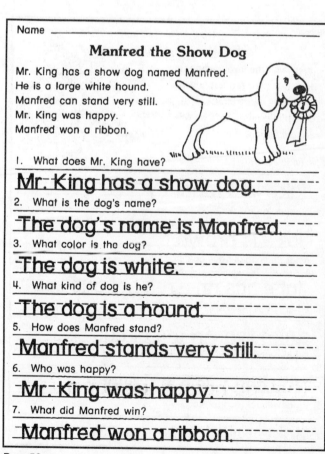

1. What does Mr. King have?

Mr. King has a show dog.

2. What is the dog's name?

The dog's name is Manfred.

3. What color is the dog?

The dog is white.

4. What kind of dog is he?

The dog is a hound.

5. How does Manfred stand?

Manfred stands very still.

6. Who was happy?

Mr. King was happy.

7. What did Manfred win?

Manfred won a ribbon.

Page 56

118

FS-32043 Reading

Answer Key

Name

The Rocket

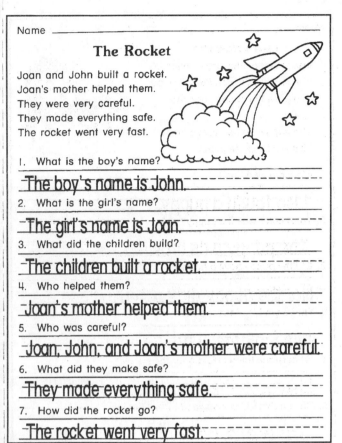

Joan and John built a rocket.
Joan's mother helped them.
They were very careful.
They made everything safe.
The rocket went very fast.

1. What is the boy's name?

The boy's name is John.

2. What is the girl's name?

The girl's name is Joan.

3. What did the children build?

The children built a rocket.

4. Who helped them?

Joan's mother helped them.

5. Who was careful?

Joan, John, and Joan's mother were careful.

6. What did they make safe?

They made everything safe.

7. How did the rocket go?

The rocket went very fast.

Page 57

Name

The Race

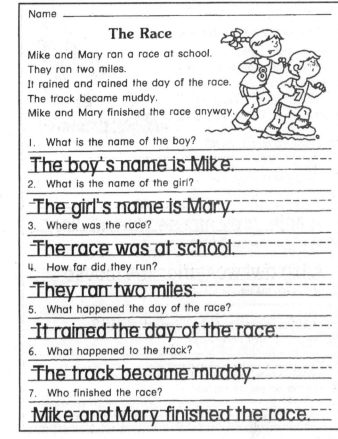

Mike and Mary ran a race at school.
They ran two miles.
It rained and rained the day of the race.
The track became muddy.
Mike and Mary finished the race anyway.

1. What is the name of the boy?

The boy's name is Mike.

2. What is the name of the girl?

The girl's name is Mary.

3. Where was the race?

The race was at school.

4. How far did they run?

They ran two miles.

5. What happened the day of the race?

It rained the day of the race.

6. What happened to the track?

The track became muddy.

7. Who finished the race?

Mike and Mary finished the race.

Page 58

Name

Summer Camp

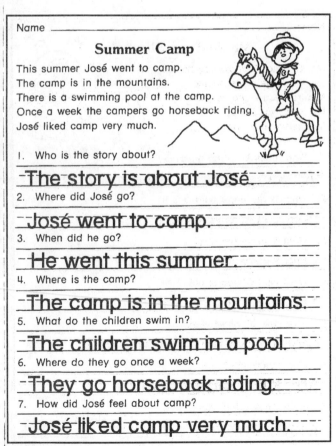

This summer José went to camp.
The camp is in the mountains.
There is a swimming pool at the camp.
Once a week the campers go horseback riding.
José liked camp very much.

1. Who is the story about?

The story is about José.

2. Where did José go?

José went to camp.

3. When did he go?

He went this summer.

4. Where is the camp?

The camp is in the mountains.

5. What do the children swim in?

The children swim in a pool.

6. Where do they go once a week?

They go horseback riding.

7. How did José feel about camp?

José liked camp very much.

Page 59

Name

Making Breakfast

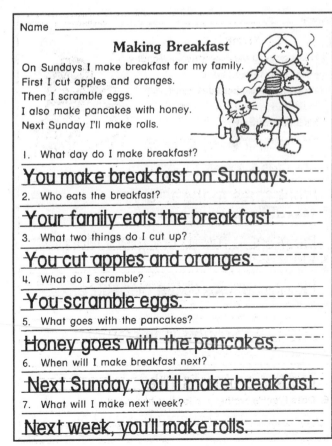

On Sundays I make breakfast for my family.
First I cut apples and oranges.
Then I scramble eggs.
I also make pancakes with honey.
Next Sunday I'll make rolls.

1. What day do I make breakfast?

You make breakfast on Sundays.

2. Who eats the breakfast?

Your family eats the breakfast.

3. What two things do I cut up?

You cut apples and oranges.

4. What do I scramble?

You scramble eggs.

5. What goes with the pancakes?

Honey goes with the pancakes.

6. When will I make breakfast next?

Next Sunday, you'll make breakfast.

7. What will I make next week?

Next week, you'll make rolls.

Page 60

FS-32043 Reading

Answer Key

Name _____

Playing Tennis

Joe learned to play tennis.
He took eight lessons.
He learned to hit the ball over the net.
His father bought him new tennis shoes.
The shoes are green and white.

1. What is the boy's name?

The boy's name is Joe.

2. What did he learn?

He learned to play tennis.

3. How many lessons did he take?

He took eight lessons.

4. Where did he learn to hit the ball?

He learned to hit the ball over the net.

5. Who bought him shoes?

His father bought him shoes.

6. Were the shoes new or old?

The shoes were new.

7. What colors are the shoes?

The shoes are green and white.

Page 61

Name _____

Across the Sea

We saw a film in school yesterday.
It was about two men who sailed across the sea.
They sailed on a raft.
They ate what they found in the water.
We thought they were brave men.

1. What did we see in school?

You saw a film.

2. When did we see it?

You saw it yesterday.

3. How many men sailed?

Two men sailed.

4. Where did they sail?

They sailed across the sea.

5. What did they sail on?

They sailed on a raft.

6. What did they eat?

They ate what they found in the water.

7. What did we think about the men?

You thought they were brave.

Page 62

Name _____

Our Team

Our baseball team won ten games.
We lost five games.
The coach says we had a good year.
The team is going to have a party on Saturday.
We will give the coach a gold cup.

1. What kind of team do we have?

You have a baseball team.

2. How many games have we won?

You have won ten games.

3. How many games have we lost?

You have lost five games.

4. Who said we had a good year?

The coach said you had a good year.

5. What is the team going to have?

The team will have a party.

6. What day is the party?

The party is on Saturday.

7. What will we give the coach?

You will give the coach a gold cup.

Page 63

Name _____

The Space Museum

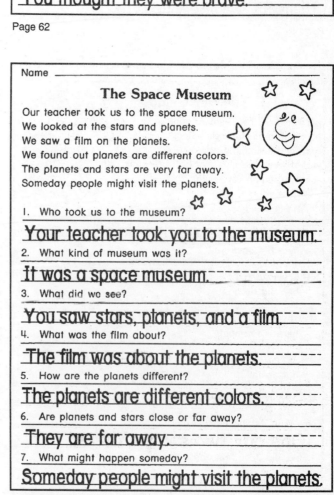

Our teacher took us to the space museum.
We looked at the stars and planets.
We saw a film on the planets.
We found out planets are different colors.
The planets and stars are very far away.
Someday people might visit the planets.

1. Who took us to the museum?

Your teacher took you to the museum.

2. What kind of museum was it?

It was a space museum.

3. What did we see?

You saw stars, planets, and a film.

4. What was the film about?

The film was about the planets.

5. How are the planets different?

The planets are different colors.

6. Are planets and stars close or far away?

They are far away.

7. What might happen someday?

Someday people might visit the planets.

Page 64

120

Answer Key

Name _____

The Gold Watch

My grandfather gave me a pocket watch.
It is made of gold.
The watch has a long chain.
A long time ago the watch belonged to my great-grandfather.
That watch is very old!
But it is still running.

1. Who gave me the watch?

Your grandfather gave you the watch.

2. What kind of watch is it?

It is a pocket watch.

3. What is the watch made of?

The watch is made of gold.

4. What does the watch have?

The watch has a long chain.

5. Who did the watch belong to a long time ago?

The watch belonged to your great grandfather.

6. Is the watch new or old?

The watch is very old!

7. What is the watch still doing?

The watch is still running.

Page 65

Name _____

Tom Turtle

Terry has a pet turtle.
His name is Tom.
Tom lives in the yard.
One day Terry lost Tom.
Tom was lost for three weeks.
She found him in the flowers.

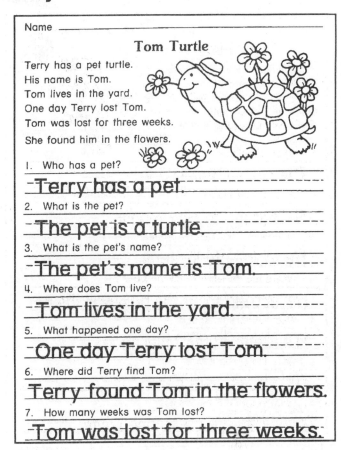

1. Who has a pet?

Terry has a pet.

2. What is the pet?

The pet is a turtle.

3. What is the pet's name?

The pet's name is Tom.

4. Where does Tom live?

Tom lives in the yard.

5. What happened one day?

One day Terry lost Tom.

6. Where did Terry find Tom?

Terry found Tom in the flowers.

7. How many weeks was Tom lost?

Tom was lost for three weeks.

Page 66

Name _____

The River

Bruce lives by the river.
The river is very big.
Ships go up the river.
Barges come down the river.
One day two ships crashed.
Now there is a hole in one.

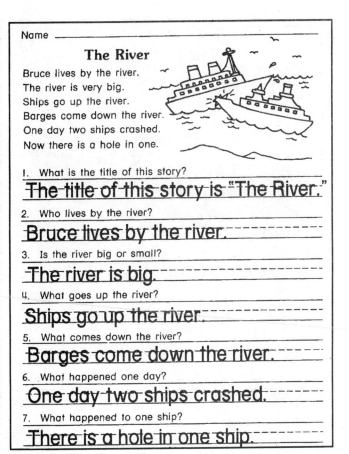

1. What is the title of this story?

The title of this story is "The River."

2. Who lives by the river?

Bruce lives by the river.

3. Is the river big or small?

The river is big.

4. What goes up the river?

Ships go up the river.

5. What comes down the river?

Barges come down the river.

6. What happened one day?

One day two ships crashed.

7. What happened to one ship?

There is a hole in one ship.

Page 67

Name _____

Zoos

Zoos have large and small animals.
The birds fly in cages.
The monkeys swing on bars.
The bears have caves.
The snakes are behind glass.
The animals are fed every day.

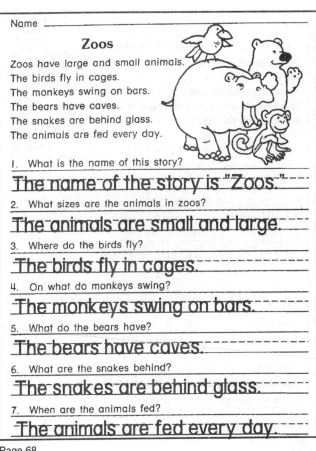

1. What is the name of this story?

The name of the story is "Zoos."

2. What sizes are the animals in zoos?

The animals are small and large.

3. Where do the birds fly?

The birds fly in cages.

4. On what do monkeys swing?

The monkeys swing on bars.

5. What do the bears have?

The bears have caves.

6. What are the snakes behind?

The snakes are behind glass.

7. When are the animals fed?

The animals are fed every day.

Page 68

FS-32043 Reading

Answer Key

Name _____

Bedtime

My bedtime is at 9 o'clock.
I go to my room at 8 o'clock.
First I read for ten minutes.
Then I brush my teeth.
After that I take a bath.
The last thing I do is put my clothes on the chair.

1. When is my bedtime?

-Your bedtime is at 9 o'clock.

2. Where do I go?

You go to your room.

3. What time do I go?

You go at 8 o'clock.

4. How long do I read?

You read for ten minutes.

5. What do I do after I read?

You brush your teeth.

6. Do I take a bath or shower?

You take a bath.

7. What is the last thing I do?

You put your clothes on the chair.

Page 69

Name _____

Ice Skating

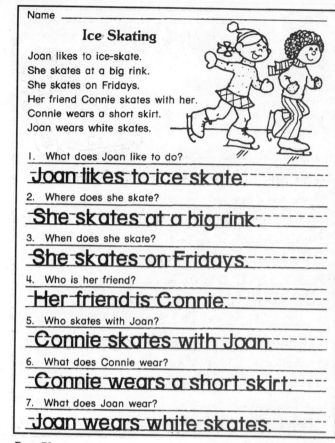

Joan likes to ice-skate.
She skates at a big rink.
She skates on Fridays.
Her friend Connie skates with her.
Connie wears a short skirt.
Joan wears white skates.

1. What does Joan like to do?

Joan likes to ice skate.

2. Where does she skate?

She skates at a big rink.

3. When does she skate?

She skates on Fridays.

4. Who is her friend?

Her friend is Connie.

5. Who skates with Joan?

Connie skates with Joan.

6. What does Connie wear?

Connie wears a short skirt.

7. What does Joan wear?

Joan wears white skates.

Page 70

Name _____

Kim's Mother

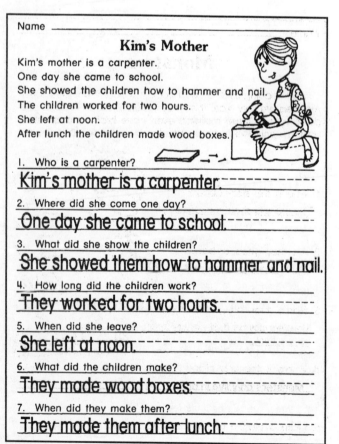

Kim's mother is a carpenter.
One day she came to school.
She showed the children how to hammer and nail.
The children worked for two hours.
She left at noon.
After lunch the children made wood boxes.

1. Who is a carpenter?

Kim's mother is a carpenter.

2. Where did she come one day?

One day she came to school.

3. What did she show the children?

She showed them how to hammer and nail.

4. How long did the children work?

They worked for two hours.

5. When did she leave?

She left at noon.

6. What did the children make?

They made wood boxes.

7. When did they make them?

They made them after lunch.

Page 71

Name _____

Bob's Party

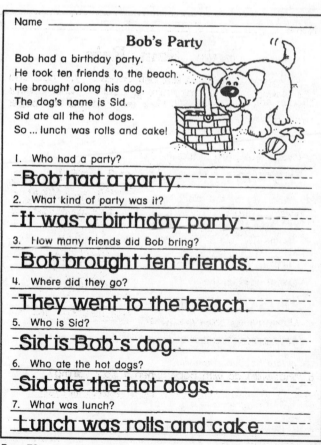

Bob had a birthday party.
He took ten friends to the beach.
He brought along his dog.
The dog's name is Sid.
Sid ate all the hot dogs.
So ... lunch was rolls and cake!

1. Who had a party?

Bob had a party.

2. What kind of party was it?

It was a birthday party.

3. How many friends did Bob bring?

Bob brought ten friends.

4. Where did they go?

They went to the beach.

5. Who is Sid?

Sid is Bob's dog.

6. Who ate the hot dogs?

Sid ate the hot dogs.

7. What was lunch?

Lunch was rolls and cake.

Page 72

Answer Key

Name _____

Our New Car

Our family has a new car.
It is silver and black.
The seats have gray stripes.
There are seat belts in the front and back.
We call our new car the Silver Star.
It goes very fast.

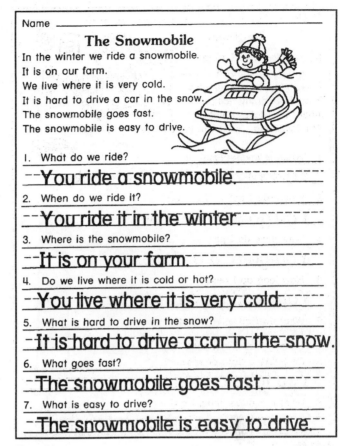

1. What is the title of the story?

The title of this story is "Our New Car."

2. Who has a new car?

Your family has a new car.

3. What colors are on the car?

The car is silver and black.

4. What color are the stripes on the seats?

The seats have gray stripes.

5. Where are the seat belts?

The seat belts are in the front and back.

6. What is the name of the car?

The name of the car is Silver Star.

7. Is the car fast or slow?

The car is fast.

Page 73

Name _____

The Snowmobile

In the winter we ride a snowmobile.
It is on our farm.
We live where it is very cold.
It is hard to drive a car in the snow.
The snowmobile goes fast.
The snowmobile is easy to drive.

1. What do we ride?

You ride a snowmobile.

2. When do we ride it?

You ride it in the winter.

3. Where is the snowmobile?

It is on your farm.

4. Do we live where it is cold or hot?

You live where it is very cold.

5. What is hard to drive in the snow?

It is hard to drive a car in the snow.

6. What goes fast?

The snowmobile goes fast.

7. What is easy to drive?

The snowmobile is easy to drive.

Page 74

Name _____

Rain, Rain, Rain

It's raining outside. No sun, only clouds . . . no boys and girls playing . . . , just rain, rain, rain. But . . . when it stops raining, I'll jump in puddles, play in the mud, and float paper boats in the street.

1. What is going on outside?

It's raining outside.

2. Is the sun out?

No, the sun is not out.

3. Are there clouds?

Yes, there are clouds.

4. Where are the boys and girls?

The boys and girls are inside.

5. What will I do with paper when it stops raining?

You will make paper boats and float them in puddles in the street.

6. Make a picture of the first sentence.

Page 75

Name _____

Monsters

I am reading such a good book. It is about monsters. These monsters are very nice. They play baseball, eat ice-cream and go to school. These monsters even have brothers and sisters. Monsters only live in books, you know. Let's keep it that way!

1. Who is this story about?

The story is about monsters.

2. Are they good or bad?

These monsters are good.

3. Name three things that monsters do.

Monsters play baseball, eat ice-cream, and go to school.

4. Where is the only place that monsters live?

Monsters only live in books.

5. Make a picture of the fourth sentence.

Page 76

Answer Key

A Mouse In Our House

There's a mouse in our house. We can't find it. We have never seen it. It eats our cheese. It makes noise at night. It makes our cat run all over the house. I hear it under my bed at night. Some day I'll see that mouse. Until then, I'll call it — Mr. Invisible!

1. Who is this story about?
   <u>This story is about a mouse.</u>

2. Where does the mouse live?
   <u>The mouse lives in your house.</u>

3. What does it eat?
   <u>It eats cheese.</u>   *Squeak!*

4. What does the cat do?
   <u>The cat runs all over the house.</u>

5. Where can I hear the mouse at night?
   <u>You can hear the mouse under your bed.</u>

6. What is the mouse's name?
   <u>The mouse's name is Mr. Invisible.</u>

7. Make a picture of the first sentence.

The Chocolate Cake Mess

Oh Oh ....! Now I did it! I put my fingers in Mother's chocolate cake. She will be mad! What will I do now? Hide in my room? No! Throw the cake away? No! Tell my mom I goofed? Right! O.K. I'll lick my fingers and go find my mother.

1. What's the problem?
   <u>You put your fingers in your Mother's chocolate cake.</u>

2. Who will be mad?
   <u>Your mother will be mad.</u>   Oh dear.

3. Name two wrong things I could do.
   <u>You could hide in your room or throw the cake away.</u>

4. What is the right thing to do?
   <u>You should tell your mom what you did.</u>

5. Why will I lick my fingers?
   <u>Answers vary.</u>

Baby-sitting

Did you ever baby-sit? Boy, it's hard work! You have to make sure the baby doesn't crawl out of the house. If he cries, you have to give him a bottle of milk. But baby-sitting is also fun. You can sure see a lot of T.V. And sometimes you can help yourself to snacks in the refrigerator.

1. What is this story about?
   <u>The story is about baby-sitting.</u>

2. Where could the baby crawl?
   <u>The baby could crawl out of the house.</u>

3. Why can baby-sitting be fun?
   <u>You can watch T.V. and eat snacks.</u>

4. What do you do if the baby cries?
   <u>You give the baby a bottle of milk.</u>

5. Draw a picture of the last sentence.

Going to the Movies

My friend Jane and I go to the movies every Saturday. We always sit up front because you can see better. Jane buys popcorn and I help her eat it. Sometimes we see a Bugs Bunny cartoon. That's all folks!

1. Where do we go on Saturday?
   <u>You go to the movies.</u>

2. Why do we sit up front?
   <u>You sit up front because you can see better.</u>

3. How do I help Jane?
   <u>You help her eat her popcorn.</u>

4. What cartoon do we see?
   <u>You see a Bugs Bunny cartoon.</u>

5. Make a picture of the first sentence.

Answer Key

Name _____

My Friend, Jimmy

It's nice to sit and talk to my friend, Jimmy. Jimmy and I tell jokes to each other. Sometimes he tells me about his monster dreams. I tell him about my pet turtle Speedy. We have learned a lot from each other.

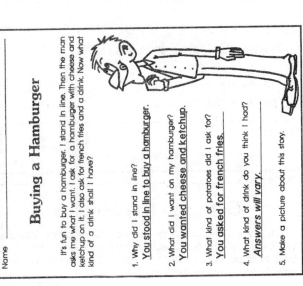

1. Who do I talk to?
   <u>You talk to Jimmy.</u>

2. What do we tell each other?
   <u>You tell each other jokes.</u>

3. What does Jimmy dream about?
   <u>Jimmy dreams about monsters.</u>

4. What is my pet called?
   <u>Your pet is called Speedy.</u>

5. Make a picture about this story.

Page 81

Name _____

Buying a Hamburger

It's fun to buy a hamburger. I stand in line. Then the man asks me what I want. I ask for a hamburger with cheese and ketchup on it. I also ask for french fries and a drink. Now what kind of a drink shall I have?

1. Why did I stand in line?
   <u>You stood in line to buy a hamburger.</u>

2. What did I want on my hamburger?
   <u>You wanted cheese and ketchup.</u>

3. What kind of potatoes did I ask for?
   <u>You asked for french fries.</u>

4. What kind of drink do you think I had?
   <u>Answers will vary.</u>

5. Make a picture about this story.

Page 82

Name _____

What Does It Mean?

Some words have the same meaning. Father and Dad . . . fast and speedy . . . sleep and snooze . . . tender and soft . . . big and large.

1. What word means the same as Father?
   <u>Dad means the same as Father.</u>

2. What word means the same as soft?
   <u>Tender means the same as soft.</u>

3. What word means the same as speedy?
   <u>Fast means the same as speedy.</u>

4. What word means the same as sleep?
   <u>Snooze means the same as sleep.</u>

5. What word means the same as big?
   <u>Large means the same as big.</u>

6. Name two other words that mean the same.
   <u>Answers will vary.</u>

Page 83

Name _____

My Bicycle

My bicycle is super. It is ten-speed and painted red. It can go so fast. I like to take long trips with my bicycle. Sometimes I honk my horn when I ride past my friend's house. I can do a trick. Sometimes I ride without my hands on the handlebars. When I go to sleep, I keep my bike next to my bed. Goodnight!

Let's go!

1. What is this story about?
   <u>The story is about your bicycle.</u>

2. What color is my bike?
   <u>Your bike is red.</u>

3. What does my friend hear when I go by?
   <u>Your friend hears your horn.</u>

4. Name a trick I can do.
   <u>You can ride without your hands on the handle bars.</u>

5. Where is my bike when I go to bed?
   <u>Your bike is next to your bed.</u>

Page 84

Name _____

Read the story.

That bird cannot fly. It has a hurt wing. I will take care of it. Then the bird will get well.

Read the sentences below. Cut them out and paste them in the right order.

1	It cannot fly.
2	One wing is hurt.
3	I will help the bird.
4	The bird will get well.

Cut.

One wing is hurt.

I will help the bird.

The bird will get well.

It cannot fly.

Page 85

Name _____

Read the story.

Mike looked at his bike. "Oh no, I have a flat tire," he said. "I will fix it now. Then I will pump up the tire."

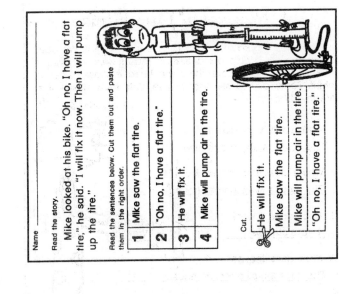

Read the sentences below. Cut them out and paste them in the right order.

1	Mike saw the flat tire.
2	"Oh no, I have a flat tire."
3	He will fix it.
4	Mike will pump air in the tire.

Cut.

He will fix it.

Mike saw the flat tire.

Mike will pump air in the tire.

"Oh no, I have a flat tire."

Page 86

125

Answer Key

Name _____

Read the story.

Nan hears a bell. She runs to get her money. Now she sees the red truck. She wants to buy ice cream.

Read the sentences below. Cut them out and paste them in the right order.

1	The bell is ringing.
2	Nan gets her money.
3	She can see the red truck.
4	Nan will buy ice cream.

Cut.

Nan gets her money.
She can see the red truck.
The bell is ringing.
Nan will buy ice cream.

Page 87

Name _____

Read the story.

"Watch me mix a new color! First I will put some white paint in the dish. Now I will add red paint. I made pink paint."

Read the sentences below. Cut them out and paste them in the right order.

1	Watch me mix a new color!
2	I will put white paint in the dish.
3	I will add red paint.
4	Look at the new color.

Cut.

I will add red paint.
Look at the new color.
I will put white paint in the dish.
Watch me mix a new color!

Page 88

Name _____

Read the story.

"I need to phone my mother. May I use your phone? I will tell Mother where I am. Then I'll ask if I may play."

Read the sentences below. Cut them out and paste them in the right order.

1	I must make a phone call.
2	May I use your phone?
3	I will tell Mom where I am.
4	I'll ask Mother if I may play.

Cut.

I will tell Mom where I am.
I'll ask Mother if I may play.
I must make a phone call.
May I use your phone?

Page 89

Name _____

Read the story.

"I can trace that," said Pam. "Put the shape on the paper. Now I will trace around it. Then I can cut it out."

Read the sentences below. Cut them out and paste them in the right order.

1	Pam said, "I can trace."
2	"Put the shape on the paper."
3	"I'll trace around the shape."
4	"Now I will cut it out."

Cut.

"I'll trace around the shape."
Pam said, "I can trace."
"Now I will cut it out."
"Put the shape on the paper."

Page 90

Name _____

Read the story.

It is the first day of school. I found my new room. The teacher said, "Hello. I'm Miss Rand." Then I sat at my desk.

Read the sentences below. Cut them out and paste them in the right order.

1	It is the first day of school.
2	I found my class.
3	The teacher said, "Hello."
4	I found my desk.

Cut.

The teacher said, "Hello."
I found my desk.
It is the first day of school.
I found my class.

Page 91

Name _____

Read the story.

Don said, "I'm riding my bike today." He rode down the street. He saw Pat on his bike. They rode to school.

Read the sentences below. Cut them out and paste them in the right order.

1	"I'm riding my bike," said Don.
2	Don rode down the street.
3	Don saw Pat.
4	Pat and Don rode to school.

Cut.

Pat and Don rode to school.
Don saw Pat.
Don rode down the street.
"I'm riding my bike," said Don.

Page 92

Answer Key

Page 95

Name

Read the story.

"It is time for your spelling test," said Mr. Green. "Write your name on the paper. Then write the numbers from one to ten. Now spell the word 'cat'."

Read the sentences below. Cut them out and paste them in the right order.

1	Mr. Green started to talk.
2	"It is time for the test."
3	"Write your name."
4	"Put numbers on your paper."
5	"Spell the word 'cat'."

Cut.

- "Write your name."
- "Spell the word 'cat'."
- Mr. Green started to talk.
- "Put numbers on your paper."
- "It is time for the 'test'."

Page 95

Page 98

Name

Read the story.

Today is my little sister's birthday. My mother is baking a cake. Then she will frost the cake. I will put three candles on the cake. Then we will sing "Happy Birthday".

Read the sentences below. Cut them out and paste them in the right order.

1	Today is my sister's birthday.
2	Mother will bake a cake.
3	She will frost the cake.
4	I will put on the candles.
5	We will sing to my sister.

Cut.

- She will frost the cake.
- We will sing to my sister.
- Mother will bake a cake.
- I will put on the candles.
- Today is my sister's birthday.

Page 98

Page 94

Name

Read the story.

I like to play soccer. My friend Ted is on my team. After school we will go to our game. Then Ted's dad will take us home.

Read the sentences below. Cut them out and paste them in the right order.

1	I like to play soccer.
2	My friend is on my team.
3	We will go to our game.
4	We will go home.

Cut.

- My friend is on my team.
- We will go to our game.
- We will go home.
- I like to play soccer.

Page 94

Page 97

Name

Read the story.

My dog sits by the door. I come home and he licks my hand. He barks and rolls over. He wants a treat. I always give him a treat after school.

Read the sentences below. Cut them out and paste them in the right order.

1	My dog sits at the door.
2	I come home from school.
3	He licks my hand.
4	He barks and rolls over.
5	I give my dog a treat.

Cut.

- I give my dog a treat.
- He barks and rolls over.
- He licks my hand.
- My dog sits at the door.
- I come home from school.

Page 97

Page 93

Name

Read the story.

Kim told Mother to look outside. The sky is getting dark. Now the wind is blowing. It is starting to rain!

Read the sentences below. Cut them out and paste them in the right order.

1	Kim told Mother to look.
2	The sky is getting dark.
3	The wind is blowing.
4	It is raining now.

Cut.

- The wind is blowing.
- Kim told Mother to look.
- It is raining now.
- The sky is getting dark.

Page 93

Page 96

Name

Read the story.

My fish are fun to watch. They hide in the grass. Then I drop in some food. They swim up to the top to eat. Then they hide in the grass again.

Read the sentences below. Cut them out and paste them in the right order.

1	I like to watch my fish.
2	The fish hide in the grass.
3	I feed the fish.
4	They swim to the top.
5	They eat and hide again.

Cut.

- I like to watch my fish.
- I feed the fish.
- The fish hide in the grass.
- They eat and hide again.
- They swim to the top.

Page 96

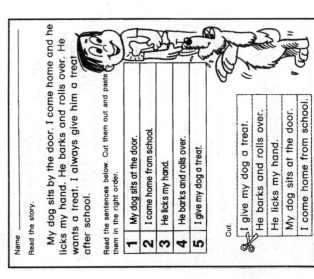

FS-32043 Reading

Answer Key

Page 101

Name ___

Read the story.

I need a book about cats. I will go to the library. Then I will find some books. I can take the books home with me. Daddy and I will read them.

Read the sentences below. Cut them out and paste them in the right order.

1 I need a book.
2 I will go to the library.
3 I will find the books.
4 I will take the books home.
5 Daddy and I will read them.

Cut.
Daddy and I will read them.
I need a book.
I will find the books.
I will go to the library.
I will take the books home.

Page 104

Name ___

Read the story.

I got my pumpkin yesterday. I marked the eyes, nose and mouth. My sister will cut it. Then I will take the seeds out. I will put the jack-o-lantern in the window.

Read the sentences below. Cut them out and paste them in the right order.

1 Now I have my pumpkin.
2 I marked the face.
3 My sister will help.
4 I will take the seeds out.
5 My jack-o-lantern is done.

Cut.
I marked the face.
I will take the seeds out.
Now I have my pumpkin.
My jack-o-lantern is done.
My sister will help.

Page 100

Name ___

Read the story.

"You got a letter in the mail," said Mother. I was surprised. I opened the letter. It was about Tom's party. I will go to the party.

Read the sentences below. Cut them out and paste them in the right order.

1 Mother told me I got a letter.
2 I was surprised.
3 I opened the letter.
4 The letter is about a party.
5 I will go to the party.

Cut.
I was surprised.
The letter is about a party.
Mother told me I got a letter.
I opened the letter.
I will go to the party.

Page 103

Name ___

Read the story.

I found a cat. It had a tag on its neck with a phone number. I called and a man came to get the lost cat. He told me it was his boy's cat.

Read the sentences below. Cut them out and paste them in the right order.

1 I found a cat.
2 I called the number.
3 I talked to a man.
4 He came to my house.
5 He took the cat.

Cut.
I called the number.
He came to my house.
He took the cat.
I found a cat.
I talked to a man.

Page 99

Name ___

Read the story.

Run home from school. Ask your mother if you can come to my house. Then ride over on your bike. We will ride bikes. Then we can play a game.

Read the sentences below. Cut them out and paste them in the right order.

1 Run home from school.
2 You must ask your mother.
3 Ride your bike to my house.
4 We will ride bikes.
5 We will play a game.

Cut.
We will ride bikes.
You must ask your mother.
We will play a game.
Ride your bike to my house.
Run home from school.

Page 102

Name ___

Read the story.

Last June I planted my seeds. A long green vine grew. Orange flowers grew on the vine. Each flower will become a pumpkin. I can give pumpkins to my friends.

Read the sentences below. Cut them out and paste them in the right order.

1 I planted some seeds.
2 A long green vine grew.
3 Then orange flowers grew.
4 The flowers will be pumpkins.
5 I will give pumpkins away.

Cut.
A long green vine grew.
The flowers will be pumpkins.
I planted some seeds.
I will give pumpkins away.
Then orange flowers grew.